LOOKING FOR FAME
THE LIFE OF A POP PRINCESS
LADY GAGA
PAUL LESTER

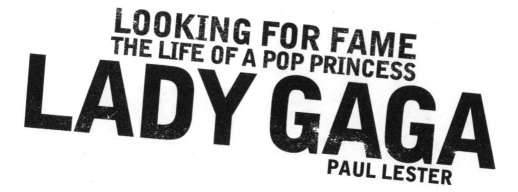

OMNIBUS PRESS

London / New York / Paris / Sydney / Copenhagen / Berlin / Madrid / Tokyo

Copyright © 2010 Omnibus Press
(A Division of Music Sales Limited)

Cover designed by Fresh Lemon
Picture research by Jacqui Black

ISBN: 978.1.84938.405.6
Order No: OP53438

Exclusive Distributors
Music Sales Limited,
14/15 Berners Street,
London, W1T 3LJ.

Music Sales Corporation,
257 Park Avenue South,
New York, NY 10010, USA.

Macmillan Distribution Services,
56 Parkwest Drive
Derrimut, Vic 3030,
Australia.

Every effort has been made to trace the copyright holders of the photographs in this book but one or two were unreachable. We would be grateful if the photographers concerned would contact us.

Typeset by: Phoenix Photosetting, Chatham, Kent
Printed in the EU

A catalogue record for this book is available from the British Library.

Visit Omnibus Press on the web at www.omnibuspress.com

Contents

Chapter 1

The Fame

"I've always lived, in New York, this very art-centric, glamorous life."

– Lady Gaga

It is March 5, 2010 and Lady Gaga is teetering towards the TV presenter in fancy designer shoes with impossibly high transparent plastic heels. She is also wearing a tight, shiny black leather trouser suit with giant flares that contrasts starkly with her long platinum blonde hair/wig, which is tinged yellow down one side and pink down the other.

It would be a fairly remarkable get-up even without the black-telephone hat that she has on her head. Even Jonathan Ross, the normally unflappable host whose British TV show Gaga is appearing on for the second time in under a year, is taken aback, despite the fact that the last time he had the pop superstar on his couch, she was wearing a radically unusual red dress made entirely out of Post-it notes.

Ross wonders aloud whether the hat-telephone – a simulation

antique affair with a removable handset presumably worn to tie in with the release of 'Telephone', the second UK single from her album *The Fame Monster* – actually works.

"Hello?" she demonstrates by talking into the receiver. "Hi, Jonathan?" she continues, as though she's sitting cosily at home and having a regular, intimate conversation with a good friend at long distance, rather than, say, with a chat-show host in front of a BBC audience and millions of television viewers. She lets the handset dangle by its cord as the interview resumes, then picks it up and holds it as though for security. Gaga looks a bit anxious and uncomfortable as she listens to a comment from Ross about her "incredible year" and parries a question about whether she was regarded at first by people as "an oddity."

"I guess so, yes," she concedes, a tad surprised to be criticised, albeit mildly, on national TV in a country that has taken to her arguably more instantly than any other, the USA included. She seems pleased when Ross then notes the change in perception towards her, from astonished amusement to adoration, since her emergence onto the world's stage mere months earlier. "Now," he says of previously sceptical onlookers, "they love what you do."

"Thank you," she says, fluttering her huge false eyelashes. "Thank you so much." She pauses, adding: "I really love my fans." There are cheers from the BBC audience.

Ross then asks Lady Gaga, in an interview that is sandwiched between performances of her ballad 'Brown Eyes' and latest single, 'Telephone', featuring Beyoncé (obviously minus the popular R&B artist), if she is concerned that the performance-art aspect of what she does, the risqué couture and shock-and-awe costumes, might somehow overshadow the music?

"I've always lived, in New York, this very art-centric, glamorous life," she explains with the faintest trace of a wry smile. "It's important to me to always be that for my fans." She admits that she doesn't want to be one of those celebrities who are photographed in their civvies, "taking out the trash". That kind of myth-debunking revelation by paparazzi is, she declares grandly, "destroying show business".

"There is," she proclaims, "absolutely no way I would give up my wigs and hats for anything." The producers of *Friday Night With Jonathan Ross* proceed to beam onscreen the famous kooky image of Gaga at the 2009 Accessories Council Excellence (ACE) Awards, where she was presented with a Stylemaker Award by arch fashionista Marc Jacobs.

That night, her incredible outfit, designed by her own personal fashion team known as the Haus Of Gaga, comprised a black button-down shirt that seemed to be covered in chalk dust, over which she wore a bullet bra – yes, the bra was over the shirt. The shirt itself was tucked into shiny high-waist silver hot pants, while the star stood there tottering on vertiginous mint-green shoes. Most outrageous of all was her headwear: a Marie Antoinette-style bouffant and a black lace veil that covered most of her face.

As soon as the image of Gaga appears on the screen, Ross' audience responds with whoops and hollers. "You're inspiring tens of thousands – hundreds of thousands – of other people to be a bit bolder, a bit brasher and more adventurous," the presenter states, admiringly, a far cry from his attitude during her appearance on his show the year before when, after goading her with the rumours surrounding her sexuality and alleged transgender characteristics, she was moved to reveal that she had a "really big donkey dick".

To shouts of support and enthusiastic clapping, Gaga tells Ross, no stranger to controversy himself following his highly publicised 'victimisation' in 2008, alongside comedian Russell Brand, of actor Andrew (Manuel from *Fawlty Towers*) Sachs: "I don't dress for the sake of being overdramatic or overexuberant." She goes on to explain that, for her, fashion is about "being whoever you want to be".

Ross then announces that Lady Gaga's début album, *The Fame*, and its associated follow-up *The Fame Monster*, have just been accorded diamond status, signifying 10 million sales worldwide. "I didn't even know you could go diamond!" he admits to wild applause, before trying to diminish the triumph by joking that many of her fans buy her CDs simply "to turn them into hats".

Ignoring him, Gaga says that she feels "so blessed" – "especially," she adds, "in the age of piracy." The rest of her visit to Ross' brown leather sofa is spent deftly fielding enquiries about her love life and her supposed lack of friends in the music industry. She refuses to talk not just about her love life but even to open up when quizzed about her hero David Bowie, her feelings towards whom she describes as "sacred".

She does, however, discuss what happened when she, the newly crowned Queen of Pop, met the Queen of England following her eccentric Royal Variety Performance in December 2009. There, she was sat on top of a 13-foot-high piano and squeezed into a bizarre scarlet latex version of an Elizabethan dress, complete with chin-hugging ruff, 20-foot train and matching red panda eye make-up. Her Majesty was, apparently, highly amused.

Finally, Ross spends a good minute or so of his allotted nine minutes teasing Gaga about her stylish apparel and devotion to fashion. She must occasionally, he suggests, go out *au naturel*, minus her striking *maquillage* and flamboyant attire, in regular baggy pants and sweatshirt. He then asks whether it would be possible for her to "come back on here one day wearing what you wear when you fall out of bed?"

Gaga, ever the lady, is unperturbed by Ross' impudence. "I look impossibly fresh when I fall out of bed," she tells him, confessing that she "would rather die than have my fans not see me in a pair of high heels". She adds: "That's showbiz!"

Lady Gaga's domination of show business, the music industry, call it what you will, is so complete that, by the spring of 2010, barely a year after first coming to widespread attention, she is possibly the most famous, and certainly the hottest, pop star on the planet, her idol and obvious antecedent Madonna included. Her reputation in the UK, to cite just one territory that has submitted to her will, is such that her every move and change of outfit are scrutinised by blogs and gossip magazines – a day after her appearance on *Friday Night With Jonathan Ross*, for example, she is photographed at Heathrow Airport apparently dressed as a human-sized PVC bee following a collision with a road chevron.

Meanwhile, a matter as routine as the release of a single and accompanying video are, because it's Gaga, treated as major events with the gravitas of serious news. "Lady Gaga's epic new video for 'Telephone' featuring Beyoncé to make its worldwide début exclusively on *E! News* [on] Thursday March 11 at 11.30pm," her record company breathlessly announce two days ahead of the premiere of a video that they promise will be "incredible" and "jaw-dropping". Her label, Universal, describes the video – directed by Jonas Åkerlund, fêted for his promos for Madonna and U2 and, especially, the infamous short that accompanied The Prodigy's 'Smack My Bitch Up' – as a "gritty, erotic and wildly fierce, nine-minute, visually stunning, cinematic masterpiece".

Universal's excitement is forgivable. This is, after all, an artist who, since her arrival on the scene in 2008, has won several prestigious Grammy awards; who has released an album – *The Fame* – that spawned a record-breaking four American number one singles in 'Just Dance', 'Poker Face', 'LoveGame' and 'Paparazzi', and issued a follow-up album called *The Fame Monster* featuring a fifth US number one ('Bad Romance'), whose video alone racked up more than 140 million views online; and who has sold a total of 27 million records, including 10 million albums and 17 million singles.

Much of the fever-pitch expectation elicited by the single is due to the accompanying visuals. Around the release of her previous single, 'Bad Romance', with its video's shocking, no-holds-barred depiction of love as disease and degradation, dominance and submission, one MTV presenter called Lady Gaga "the scariest person on our chart". The signs are that, with 'Telephone', she might have exceeded herself.

Certainly a sneak preview of some stills from the video ahead of the actual premiere suggests it will be as arresting as the one for 'Bad Romance'. In one of them Gaga is wearing heavy-duty chains and sci-fi cyber sunglasses made out of – of all things – cigarettes; in another she's naked except for some yellow-and-black tape, of the type that police use at crime scenes; in another she's wearing a stars-and-stripes bikini; and in another she resembles a heavy metal housewife in her leather jacket covered in studs and hair in rollers made out of Diet Coke cans.

Lady Gaga said of the premiere: "What I like about it is it's a real true pop event. When I was younger I was always excited when there was a big, giant event happening in pop music and that's what I wanted this to be."

It has been a month or so of "big, giant events" for keen Lady Gaga watchers. At the BRITs in February 2010 she won awards for International Album, International Breakthrough Act and International Female Solo Artist and stole the show with a variety of 'outfits' – the term used advisedly because they included one of her dressed as a wedding cake and another, admittedly only worn backstage, that involved nothing but newspaper cuttings to cover her modesty.

According to Alexis Petridis of *The Guardian*: "She was the solitary bright spot at a tedious BRIT Awards ceremony. Arriving midway, apparently wearing a proportion of the set on her head and performing a ballad dedicated to Alexander McQueen [who died the week before], she seemed like the only real pop star present; certainly *X Factor*-sponsored boy band JLS, dangling precariously from wires over the stage, looked a bit wan by comparison."

Also in February, at the *NME* Awards, Gaga bizarrely manages to win in both the best-dressed and worst-dressed pop star categories (with special mention made of her outfit made entirely out of Kermit the Frog dolls).

But no event is as big, giant even, as Lady Gaga's brief Monster Ball UK tour in February and March. At the MEN arena in Manchester, the live spectacular finds her writhing on the floor of the stage as she is attacked by a monstrous undersea creature, all teeth and tentacles. At various points thereafter the Gaga extravaganza includes flaming pianos, some pretend green vomit spurted from the mouth of a woman in a negligee, some simulated group masturbation, and a series of costume changes that, by all accounts, involve the shoulder pads becoming increasingly immense. It is, decides Kitty Empire in her *Observer* review, "a performance of truly gargantuan proportions".

Petridis of *The Guardian* is also at the MEN, where he remarks that so great now is Lady Gaga's celebrity, so awesome her star power, that she can reduce an audience to paroxysms of excitement simply by removing her sunglasses, as she does halfway through one song. The journalist then notes the £50 hoodies for sale over at the merchandise stall emblazoned with the slogan "I LOVE LADY GAY GAY". He estimates that, among the teenage boys in the crowd with hair sprayed with glitter and faces festooned with Gaga-via-Bowie's trademark *Aladdin Sane*-era lightning flash make-up, there will probably be a few Manchester rough boys from local estates bound to have their preconceptions challenged, and orientations changed, on this special night.

"Lady Gaga," Petridis marvels, "might actually be that rarest of things: a pop star who encourages the audience to take risks, invites their fans not merely to listen to their music and buy their records, but enter into a kind of alternate world."

That alternate world, that parallel reality, which Lady Gaga rules like a benign despot, has been in existence a mere two years. It seems to have come from nowhere and taken shape overnight. But Gaga's world, like her fame, had a considerable gestation period, and very earthly beginnings.

Chapter 2

Pre-Fame

"I was always an entertainer. I was a ham as a little girl and I'm a ham today."

– Lady Gaga

She may have the alien allure of someone who was beamed down from a distant planet sometime in the middle of the first decade of the 21st century, but Lady Gaga's back-story is far less out-of-the-ordinary than that.

In fact, she was born Stefani Joanne Angelina Germanotta, in Yonkers, New York, on March 28, 1986. Of her Italian-American parents, her father, Joseph, was an internet entrepreneur from New Jersey, while her mother, Cynthia (whose original family name was Bissett), worked in telecommunications.

The family was well-off, living on the Upper West Side of Manhattan; as a consequence the Germanottas could afford to send their eldest daughter (the younger Natali was born six years after her sister) to a good school: the Convent of the Sacred Heart, the oldest independent girls' school in Manhattan, reputed to cost around £23,000 a year and whose previous alumni include Caroline Kennedy, daughter of the late President Kennedy.

Stefani's parents had originally intended to send her to a different, though equally prestigious, seat of learning: the Juilliard School, located at the Lincoln Center for the Performing Arts in New York City, where such notables as Kelsey Grammar, Val Kilmer, Kevin Spacey and Christopher Reeve were once pupils.

It was Stefani's musical and theatrical bent that had led Joseph and Cynthia to consider Juilliard as an option. At kindergarten she had entertained parents and teachers, and her peers, with her spirited performance as the big billy-goat in the *Three Billy Goats Gruff*. She even displayed early signs of DIY invention when she made the goat's horns out of tinfoil and a hanger.

Aged four, encouraged by her mother, she began taking piano lessons and before long she was able to play by ear. She even wrote her very first song, a little ditty entitled 'Dollar Bills' inspired by Pink Floyd's 'Money'. "I still remember the first song I heard," Lady Gaga later recalled. "My dad was listening to what I now know was Pink Floyd's 'Money', and understanding only the sounds of the cash register in the intro, I wrote a song called 'Dollar Bills' on my Mickey Mouse staff paper."

As she explains on her official website, when she was a little girl she would sing along to the hits of Michael Jackson and Cyndi Lauper that she could play on her mini plastic tape recorder. She would also get "twirled in the air in daddy's arms" to the raucous pop of The Rolling Stones and The Beatles.

Her father introduced her to myriad types of music, from Frank Sinatra to Bruce Springsteen. She told *Blender* magazine: "I'm a New York Italian. My father used to play Pink Floyd, Led Zeppelin, The Beatles, Billy Joel and Elton John records all the time on the record player in the living room. So music was a big part of my family. We'd listen to Andrea Bocelli and Frank Sinatra over dinner. Theatre became a huge part of my life because of that."

Joseph even played in a bar band in his spare time, so that he could give full rein to his Springsteen infatuation. Such a fan was he of the Boss that, years later, when Stefani had metamorphosed into Lady Gaga and had been given a high-profile slot at the 2009 Glastonbury Festival alongside Springsteen, she surmised that her father would doubtlessly rather watch New Jersey's finest than his own daughter's set. "If my dad knew that Bruce was playing Glastonbury, he'd fly over and he'd probably totally ignore my set and barge his way to the front to see the Boss," she said. "If you're from Jersey, then [Springsteen] is like God."

The young Stefani Germanotta would take every opportunity to engage passers-by with her musical and theatrical routines. As it says on www.ladygaga.com, "The precocious child would dance around the table at fancy Upper West Side restaurants using the breadsticks as a baton. And she would innocently greet a new babysitter in nothing but her birthday suit."

In other words, there were signs, even this early, of the flamboyant, exhibitionist adult that the world recognises today as Lady Gaga. Even the area where she grew up – the West Seventies – is one that she has referred to as "Manhattan's theatre and opera district". "I was always an entertainer," she has said. "I was a ham as a little girl and I'm a ham today."

This is precisely why the arts and entertainment-based Juilliard was deemed the ideal school for the 11-year-old Stefani Germanotta. However, at the last minute, the decision was made to send her to the Convent of the Sacred Heart – reports vary as to whether this was her parents' decision, or that of the wilful young Gaga herself. Not that the Convent was an entirely inappropriate second choice – it was, after all, the school attended by Paris Hilton and her sister Nicky. She has talked about the indirect impact the Hiltons had on her. "They're very pretty, and very clean," she told a reporter. "Very, very clean. You know, I never saw Paris, she was older than me, and it's funny that the press

11

always write that I went to school with the Hilton sisters, but I actually only went with Nicky. Paris, I believe, left and went to Dwight [another New York school]. But, you know, it's impressive to be that perfect all the time, these girls. I was always a weird girl in school, who did theatre and came to school with lots of red lipstick on or my hair perfectly curled, or whatever I was doing to get attention. It's funny as it's almost like they were there to make me aware, because so much of what I do now is that I try to twist my world into the commercial community. So I guess they've been quite an influence on me. Not them in particular, but the idea of the self-proclaimed artist."

The uniform at Sacred Heart of kilt skirts had quite an impact on her, too, and possibly gave Stefani her first taste of fashion. It was something of a fashion-conscious school, or at least one populated by pupils with a penchant for fashion. "The prom was like a Ralph Lauren runway," she once said. "There were some quite privileged young ladies in attendance." It wasn't as though Stefani and her schoolmates were a perfect match, however, as she told Hattie Collins of *The Sunday Times*: "I was the arty girl, the theatre chick. I dressed differently and I came from a different social class from the other girls. I was more of an average schoolgirl..."

And yet she has always maintained that the school allowed her to indulge her creative side while simultaneously instilling in her the values of drive, determination and discipline. Alongside lessons in core curricular subjects such as English, maths and French and more modern classes in sex education and computer studies, she was able to take courses in piano, voice and drama.

"I went to a lovely school and I got an incredible education," she told Laura Barton of *The Guardian* in 2009. "And I actually think that my education is what sets me apart, cos I'm very smart. They," she said of the nuns who were her teachers, "taught me how to think. I really know how to think."

It has been suggested that the school, a series of mansion houses set in privileged surrounds, complete with marble and gold-leafed cherubs, was the inspiration for *Gossip Girl*, the ITV drama that delves into "the scandalous lives of Manhattan's elite" and the various narcotic and sexual habits of the region's affluent teens. Whether it was or not, no school, no matter how much it drives home the importance of religion and morality, can keep its pupils in check all of the time, especially out of hours.

And yet for all that, Stefani was actually a diligent student. She did behave herself, at least in her first couple of years there, with only the odd example of effrontery, such as rolling up her school skirt to make herself look sexier. She devoted herself as much to her academic lessons as she did to those areas of the curriculum that allowed her to express herself musically – she would get good grades while also taking part in school plays and carol concerts. No matter how outrageous she is considered to be today, back then she was, as far as her classmates were concerned, as down-to-earth as they come.

"Stefani is a good girl, really sweet and normal," said Cristina Civetta, a New York writer and fashion designer, speaking to the *Daily Mail* in 2009. She compared and contrasted the future Gaga – a "straight-A student who wore her skirt to her knee" – with a damaged, falling superstar like Britney Spears, concluding that, because she wasn't from a dysfunctional family, she "wouldn't burn out like Britney". Sacred Heart, Civetta claimed, was a "rich kids' school but with good morals". It might have monitored the length of girls' skirts with a yardstick, but it encouraged ambition and gave its pupils a solid grounding as well as the will to succeed: "It taught us to be very disciplined, very strong, successful women in whatever we chose as our careers, and she," Civetta added of her famous friend, "has chosen to be a performer."

Early signs of Stefani's more experimental, and naughtier, inclinations, indicating that she might indeed become a performer, came when she was in her teens. It was when she turned 13 that she first got into fashion and discovered the joys of music composition – she wrote her first song since she was a child, a ballad called 'To Love Again', that year – and the pleasure of public performance. At first she adopted a sort of mix'n'match approach to style, juxtaposing different genres and eras with utter abandon.

"I wore acid wash jeans, tank tops, sneakers… kind of Fifties, kind of clubby," she said later on. "But I'd mix it up: some days I'd be in fishnets with bright red lips."

Around the same time as her first forays into fashion, the teenage Gaga, ever precocious, made her tentative first steps towards the stage, playing at famous Greenwich Village clubs such as The Bitter End, to which she would have to be chaperoned by her supportive mother.

"These were jazz bars not sex clubs," she said by way of reassurance, speaking to Fiona Sturges of *The Independent*. "They would have open-mic nights, so my mother would take me along and say to the manager, 'Listen, I know she's too young to be in here, and I'm too old to be in here, but she's incredibly talented and she's a singer-songwriter, so can she sign up on your open-mic list, and I'll sit with her as she plays?' So we just sat and waited round for them to call my name."

As evidence of her eclecticism, even at this early stage – she was as enthusiastic about the hard rock of Led Zeppelin as she was the jazzy MOR of Judy Garland – simultaneous to these nightclub appearances Stefani sang in a band that performed cover versions of classic rock tracks by the likes of Led Zeppelin, Pink Floyd, U2 and Jefferson Airplane. Quite apart from allowing her to get her musical rocks off, she did have an ulterior motive for joining the group.

"I met some good-looking guys with guitars," she admitted to Brian Hiatt of *The Observer*, "and I wanted to have sex with really hot older men – they were seniors."

According to Gaga, looking back on her adolescence, she was always in bands of one type or another, or rehearsing for a musical at school, which helped the otherwise self-styled "artsy, nerdy girl", whose role models included David Bowie and Boy George, make more friends. But the fact that she was so driven, and so gregarious, earned her as many enemies as friends.

"I didn't really fit in," she said, "but I had friends because I'm a nice girl and fun to party with." Gaga described herself in high school as "very dedicated, very studious, very disciplined" but also "a bit insecure" as she told one interviewer: "I used to get made fun of for being either too provocative or too eccentric, so I started to tone it down. I didn't fit in, and I felt like a freak."

The other word her classmates used to describe her was "dramatic" because she was always in a play of some sort, or a musical, or a band, or some coffee shop performance. Really, though, her whole life was providing her with opportunities to perform, and her mother was her ally. "My mum taught me to dress like a lady," she said. "I'd always have big hair and red lips." To *The London Paper* she said of her schooldays: "I was a wild one. I was pretty bad in high school. I used to get in trouble for wearing raunchy clothes with my uniform. My father really thought I had a screw loose in my brain."

Her schoolmates were often hostile towards her as a result of her flamboyance, and felt anger at her "crazy socks and shoes" and matching "crazy hair". "The girls at school would be like, 'What are you, a dyke? It's only women here, why are you dressed up?'" She couldn't help being a bit of a coquette. "I dressed in this super-sexualised way," she told *Vogue* magazine. "Miniskirts, hooker boots... But because I got straight As, the teachers couldn't do anything."

A chance encounter, when she was 13, with the nephew of a famous voice coach proved to be the catalyst that would spark the next phase in her life, help stem any feelings of freakishness and give her the space to be her extrovert self.

There she was, singing 'I Want It That Way' by The Backstreet Boys in a boutique near her home in downtown New York, when the store owner, coincidentally also a musician by the name of Evan, impressed by her singing voice, pulled her aside and slipped a phone number into her hand.

"He asked me if I was a singer," she recalled later. "I was 12 or 13 and he didn't get what I was doing in a boutique of all places after school. It was just one of those really random moments when he told me that I had a really great voice."

The phone number that Evan slipped into Stefani's hand belonged to his uncle, a world-famous voice coach called Don Lawrence whose numerous clients included everyone from En Vogue to Annie Lennox. Stefani remembers calling him up and Lawrence reciting a list of his more famous pupils, including Christina Aguilera, Bono of U2 and Mick Jagger. "As the list got larger," she related, "I got more excited."

That phone call would provide the first step on her journey to The Fame.

Chapter 3

Bare Necessity

"I think I was a little nervous about going out on my own after high school."

– Lady Gaga

Don Lawrence was, apart from her beloved parents and the teachers at Sacred Heart, arguably the person who exerted the biggest influence on Stefani Germanotta in her early teens. She has described him variously as her 'guru' and 'mentor'. As she wrote in the liner notes to her début album, *The Fame*: "You are the greatest and most gifted teacher I ever had. Thank you for my voice, my work ethic, and my discipline."

It was Lawrence who, apart obviously from helping to improve her vocal technique, encouraged her to start writing music when she was barely in her teens, on the piano in her house – big-voiced ballads, the sort of showcases for melismatic pyrotechnics that you might hear on a Leona Lewis record. This in turn gave her the confidence to start performing live at local coffee houses. In fact, newly emboldened, she opened her own coffee house at high school, just so that she would have a place to play!

Throughout this period, when many parents might frown upon a child whose obsession with music could be proving a distraction from the serious matter of school work, Joseph and Cynthia Germanotta were both very supportive of their daughter, even when it looked as though her passion for performing might become less of a hobby and more of a calling.

They could see where her life was heading, and what career she might want to pursue, and so, when she was 17, after graduating from Sacred Heart, they decided that Stefani should continue her studies at New York University's Tisch School of the Arts. A sort of US equivalent of the BRITs School in South London, Tisch boasts an incredible array of stellar ex-pupils including Woody Allen, Whoopi Goldberg, Angelina Jolie, Martin Scorsese and Anne Hathaway.

It is a considerable honour for anyone to be accepted into Tisch. It is an even greater accolade to get a place there ahead of schedule. But this is what happened to Stefani Germanotta when, aged just 17, she became one of only 20 people in its 45-year history to gain early admission to the NYU arts school. There, she studied music and theatre at the Undergraduate Department of Drama, and took classes in art history and set design, both of which would stand her in good stead when she became Lady Gaga. Dancing for five hours every morning, acting and singing in the afternoon, followed by lessons on literature and modern art – "all kinds of nerdy stuff that I'm into," as she put it – provided her with the background, and the discipline, to make the music and stage the shows that she later would do as Gaga.

Even though she wouldn't be there very long, Stefani made a sizeable impact at Tisch. First, there was her attention to the demands of the curriculum. She was obviously a keen student, albeit an erratic one who was starting to show signs of being something of a free-thinking libertarian. Nevertheless, when she applied herself, she demonstrated an intelligence unusual for a burgeoning pop star. On her official website she has reprinted an essay she wrote in 2004 about art and its impact on the human body and the (social) body politic. While it finds the teenager trying to express ideas that are clearly way beyond her and using language that she doesn't quite understand ("The analysis of form, while an engaging arc to follow, can also reveal an inverse exploration of the body," she writes at one point), there is a passage where she talks about human and societal deformity and cites French renaissance writer Michel De Montaigne's essay 'Of A Monstrous Child'. Here you can detect the kernel of an idea that would later be more fully realised on her album *The Fame Monster*.

Stefani was also making an impression on the Tisch authorities for the way she could keep up with the heavy college workload while at the same time maintaining a relatively steady flow of after-hours gigs around the city. But she didn't just isolate her budding performance skills to open-mic nights; she also competed in, and almost inevitably won, an annual talent contest called Ultra Violet Live (held to benefit local cancer charities), in the process beating students from all over New York University.

So busy – almost to the point of hyperactive – was she during this period that it was hard to tell one extracurricular project from another, but Stefani is also said to have become involved, around this time, with a glam band. She provided the vocals, but not content to take such a relatively subsidiary role, she also started to write and play piano-heavy solo songs that apparently bore the influence of an array of artistes, from Tori Amos to Otis Redding, The Beatles to Elton John and Queen.

One of Gaga's most important early collaborators and something of a face on the New York club scene, Lady Starlight surprisingly found these showy ballads to her liking. "They were my favourite," she told *The Observer*, "the incredibly theatrical and emotional stuff where you could really hear her voice." You can hear that voice in full effect on YouTube, in footage of Stefani at New York University, where she sang two songs, 'Captivated' and 'Electric Kiss', the sort you could imagine any *X Factor* finalist doing a serious number on.

And yet for all these opportunities to express herself and follow her muse, Stefani still felt stifled at Tisch, and wasn't convinced that the best way to explore her love of music, theatre and art was within its walls. One of her problems was that, as far as she was concerned, she never truly fitted in there. "It never actually clicked for me in terms of art," she said, "[even though] I always knew I'd have a life in art." It was looking more and more unlikely that she would make it to the end of her course, and becoming apparent that she partly went there simply because it seemed like the right thing to do. "I think I was a little nervous about going out on my own after high school," she admitted. "It was like my family wouldn't let me take off. It was frowned upon in school to not go to college."

It was while she was at Tisch, especially when she was auditioning for some part or other, that she began to notice the trouble her contemporaries, and the college's staff, had trying to work out where she fitted in, even back then. It became something of an issue. People, she remarked, would tell her, "You're too pop" or "You're too rock" or "You're too brunette". They would say, "You're a character, you're not an artist" or, more obtusely, "It's like you're not white, but you're a stale cracker." She surmised: "I'm a weird chick, you know? Whenever I would do pop performances, people would say I should do theatre. When I would audition for musicals, they'd tell me I was too pop."

And so she took the decision to drop out of college after just one year there. The reason she gave was simply that: "I like what I like. I don't like what I don't like." In other words, she said, "Fuck it. I will do whatever I want to do." She announced her decision to her parents on her 19th birthday, telling them as politely as she could, but in no uncertain terms, that she could survive without them or their money. "I just said, 'I'm going to get an apartment and a job." Her parents took it reasonably well under the circumstances. "My mother started crying. My father was like, 'If you don't make something happen within a year, you have to go back to school.'"

She went into detail regarding her feelings about Tisch in *Wound* magazine. "I really didn't like the school," she said. "It was like a sausage factory. It was about making everybody good at lots of things rather than being amazing at one thing and sucking at all the others, which is what I'm kind of into." She explained that she would rather excel at one thing and struggle with others. She reiterated her point about causing confusion during auditions. "What was happening was I would go to musical auditions and they would say, 'You're too pop'. Or I would be playing shows and people from record labels would be there because they'd heard about the girl from Rivington Street [her favourite NYC hangout] but they would say, 'You're awesome but you're a bit too theatre'. So I was like, I'm losing either way here for whatever reason. And I really didn't care because at the end of the day I really believed in what I was doing. So instead of trying to be theatre or trying to be pop I decided to do something that married the two worlds and something that I really loved."

Pop and theatre? That sounded suspiciously like burlesque performance, which was precisely what Stefani ended up doing in the weeks and months following her departure from Tisch. But first she had to find a place to live, which she promptly did – Clinton Street, off East Broadway and part of New York's Lower East Side. She declared that her intention was to "become an artist", which was all well and good, but in the meantime, having bid farewell to her parents and let go of their purse strings, she was going to need money to live, pay the rent and buy food. So she found herself a day job waitressing at the Cornelia Street Café, while nights were spent go-go dancing at burlesque bars like the Slipper Room, and performing at clubs like the Knitting Factory in a Seventies-style revue with her friend and DJ, Lady Starlight.

"I started playing at the Lower East Side, then all over New York, really," said the artiste who was still, albeit for not much longer, known as Stefani Germanotta. She remembers being as good at waiting tables as she was at entertaining punters in skimpy stage-wear. "I was really good at it," she says of her stint at the Cornelia Street Café. "I always got big tips. I always wore heels to work! I told everybody stories, and for customers on dates, I kept it romantic. It was kind of like performing."

As for her night-time mode of employment, the actual extent of the burlesque-ness of it all changes from report to report. She termed what she did "performance art parties" in *The London Paper*. As far as she told Louise Gannon of the *News Of The World's Fabulous* magazine, what she was actually doing in clubs around this time was working as a stripper.

"I have a strong sense of my own sexuality," she said, without shame. "I love the naked human body and I have huge body confidence. I was working in strip clubs when I was 18." She did, however, acknowledge that girls from her background "weren't meant to turn into someone like me". She continued: "I come from a wealthy Italian family and went to a good school. You're meant to live with mom and dad until they die. I went against all I was brought up to be: I moved out of home, wouldn't take any help from my parents. My act was pretty wild. I'd wear black leather and dance to Black Sabbath, Guns N' Roses and Faith No More. Very rock'n'roll." Very freeing, too, although less so for her parents. "I discovered a real personal freedom through it [but] obviously my parents didn't like it. I was drawing huge crowds, setting hairspray alight onstage and dancing madly. My dad thought I'd lost it."

True enough, Joseph Germanotta was none too impressed to see his first-born cavorting about in dive bars with drag queens and go-go dancers. "He couldn't look at me for a few months," admitted Stefani, who recalls one of her choicer outfits as a "leopard-thong-fringed bikini with a sequined high waist belt and granny panties", so risqué it shocked her father to tears. "It was hard for him – he just didn't understand." Fortunately, there would be a happy ending to this saga – one day. "My parents saw me getting better, and now my father cries when he sees me perform."

Even so, to Stefani this formative stage in her career was crucial to her development as an artist, as she told *more!* magazine: "I loved being a stripper. To me it was all about the act, it was all about art. I wanted to be the most outrageous performer on that stage. I was very into heavy metal. People would come to the clubs just to see what I was going to do that night – I found the whole thing amazing. I found the idea of taking my clothes off onstage incredibly liberating. I have absolutely no problem with my sexuality and any woman who wants to get more confident about her body should try stripping because it just makes you understand the power your body has."

But it was the power of her parents that lingered. "I wasn't worried that they were watching me. I wanted them to see what I was doing. But my dad thought I was going crazy. He really thought I had lost it and he was so upset. That totally freaked me out – I didn't want to be a failure in his eyes."

Still, this was nothing compared to the dismay he would feel when he found out what his daughter was getting up to next.

Chapter 4

Dance In The Dark

"It was one of the most difficult times in my life, but it was important for me to experience, since it unlocked parts of my brain."

— Lady Gaga

Whether it was to satisfy a deep-seated craving for narcotics or to walk, albeit briefly, on the wild side previously trodden by her heroes, Stefani Germanotta's move out of the family home when she was 19 coincided with a period of alleged drug use. It is said that the future pop sensation used to spend hours imbibing intoxicants alone in her Lower East Side apartment, and the only thing that stopped her from doing so, depending on which report you believe, was her own will power, the fear of disappointing her father or the memory of a dead relative.

It wasn't just family who were concerned about Stefani's drug use. Her friends also became worried about her increasingly erratic behaviour, holed up as she was for long periods indoors. They would beg her to come out and spend time with them.

"I didn't think there was anything wrong with me until my

friends came over and said, 'Are you doing this alone?'" she recalled. "'Um, yes. Me and my mirror.'"

Her mirror? This was probably a none-too-subtle reference to drug paraphernalia. She has described these as her "coke years", making light of the fact that her life threatened to spiral out of control as a result of her indulgence, which began around 2005.

"It was quite sick," she admitted to *The Observer*, explaining that this was where the "vanity", as she put it, of her début album, *The Fame*, came from. She described her extended drugged-out sojourns in her apartment as "this very special moment that I had with myself where I could feel confident and feel like a star".

Specifically, the stars she wanted to feel like were the artists that she admired from rock history, or people like Andy Warhol, and she seemed to truly believe that the only way to achieve their level of greatness was to mimic the life that they led at their creative peak. She estimated that sustained drug use would grant her access – be the portal – to a higher state of artistic consciousness.

"I never really did the drugs for the high," she confessed to the website ShockHound. "It was more the romanticism of Andy Warhol and all the artists that I loved. I wanted to be them, and I wanted to live their life, and I wanted to understand the way that they saw things and how they arrived at their art. And I believed the only way I could do this was to live the lifestyle, and so I did. So it wasn't about getting high – it was about being an artist. About waking up in the morning at 10:30 and doing a bunch of lines and writing a bunch of music, and staying up for three days on a creative whirlwind and then panic-attacking for a week after. It was one of the most difficult times in my life, but it was important for me to experience, since it unlocked parts of my brain. But I wouldn't encourage people to do it for that reason – you can arrive at all those things on your own."

Her experience in the world of narcotics was "very deep".

As she told one journalist: "There were drugs. Serious drugs." And it came with its very own theme music. Apparently, her "soundtrack" during this phase of her life came courtesy of goth-pop overlords The Cure. "I would lock myself in my room and listen to 'Never Enough' on repeat while I did cocaine," she revealed. "I loved all their music, but I listened to this one song over and over." However, throughout it all she managed to be active and constructive. "I wasn't a lazy drug addict," she said, explaining that she would busy herself making demo tapes of the songs that she had been writing, and take them round to record companies on her bike, pretending to be her own manager if they asked who she was at reception. Other times she would spend the money accrued while waitressing or burlesque dancing on Xeroxes for posters of herself in an effort to get gigs.

In a way, it all sounds quite romantic: the budding starlet tantalised – tormented – by visions of stardom, sequestered in not-so-splendid isolation in her ramshackle apartment, enjoying vivid dreams of a life only just beyond reach. No wonder she has admitted on more than one occasion that she sometimes looks back on these dark days in her dingy NYC flat with as much fondness as regret.

Then again, just as vivid are her memories of the night she believed her drug-taking might seriously escalate. She has expressed her concern about discussing the subject too openly for fear of "inspiring", if that's the right word, other people to follow the same path – "I don't like to talk about what I did," she has said, "because I don't want to glorify it in any way. I did what I did because that's what I was doing back then." She isn't the only one to feel pangs of anxiety at revealing all about her dark night of the soul – her record company these days gets distinctly uncomfortable whenever the subject is raised. "The label gets mad at me for talking about it – they say, 'We don't want people to think that you're not a pop star.' But I am a pop star. I'm a pop star with a story!"

And so it was that she told *The Sunday Times Culture* of her terrifying ordeal when she thought she'd taken her drug exploration too far: "I had a scary experience one night and thought I might die." She added that there was one major benefit from the whole sorry saga: it gave her the biggest wake-up call of her young life. "I woke up, [and] it helped me to become the person I am. I see things in quite a fragmented, psychotic manner, which I think is because of that. But I decided it was more important to become a centred, critical thinker. That was more powerful than the drug itself."

Also powerful was her determination not to fall under the spell of hard drugs for the rest of her life, because that would be a barrier to the stardom she so desired. "I didn't go to Alcoholics Anonymous or Narcotics Anonymous," she said. "I did it myself. I have such a fear of failure; I didn't want anything to make me fail. So I stopped." She added in an interview with *more!* magazine: "I have the most incredible will power, and I decided that nothing would happen to me if I carried on like that and I wanted something to happen." She admitted that "underneath all the wildness", and despite the stripping, burlesque dancing and druggy experimentation, she was still really just Stefani from the block. "I am still the well-brought-up nice girl and I wanted to succeed. I wanted to prove myself as an artist so I put myself back on track."

If The Cure provided the soundtrack for her drug melodrama, then Edith Piaf inadvertently offered the ideal song for the aftermath of that time in Stefani's life, because as far as the future Gaga was concerned it was a clear case of 'Non, Je Ne Regrette Rien'.

"I'm glad I did it all so young, because now I'm done with it," she said, going on to explain: "At the time it was like self-discovery and a way for me to feel good about myself. But I don't want my fans to think that way; I want them to listen to my music." She said that was what the Monster Ball (the name she would later ascribe to her tour in the wake of the success of her albums *The Fame* and *The Fame Monster*) was all about – "For those who feel like a freak inside, come to my show."

One of the other reasons Lady Gaga gave for not succumbing to drug addiction was quite freaky – the thought of her late aunt, Joanne, Joseph Germanotta's sister, who died when she was 19. "I realised Joanne had instilled her spirit in me," Gaga has said. "She was a painter and a poet – and I had a spiritual vision that I had to finish her business." She insisted that Aunt Joanne continued to exert a big influence on her and her career. "I never met her," she explained, "but she's been one of the most important figures in my life."

Ultimately, though, it was her father who set her back on the straight and narrow – if, indeed, that is a term you can legitimately ascribe to a performer renowned all over the world for writhing around in videos and in concerts in varying stages of undress and generally pushing the envelope with regard to performance and sexuality in the 21st century. It was Joseph Germanotta who made her see the error of her ways, who made her accept that there was no future in trying to pretend she was some sort of tortured avant-garde waif in Andy Warhol's Factory, even if part of her was pleased that, for the sake of her muse, she endured what she did.

She told Laura Barton of *The Guardian*: "I thought I was slick as fuck, but he [Joseph] was like, 'You're fucking up, kid.' So I stopped. I didn't stop completely but I stopped for a while completely. And I would never fall into the hole that I did at that time. How deep was the hole? I kind of feel you're in or you're out with that shit, any hole is deep. I was just being nostalgic and creative and thought that I was Edie Sedgwick and making music… I dunno, I wouldn't necessarily encourage anyone to do it, but I do think that when you struggle, that's when your art gets great."

She continued to US website ShockHound, recalling the moment her father found her, high on drugs: "I looked at him and thought, 'How does he know that I'm high right now?' [But] he never said a word about the drugs, not one word. He just said, 'I just wanna tell you that anyone you meet while you're like this, and any friend that you make in the future while you are with this thing, you will lose.' And we never talked about it again."

It didn't take much to convince her that her dad was right – after all, the buzz was not quite as great as it had been when she started. Not that she became some sort of stay-at-home party pooper instead – she still liked to enjoy herself. It was just that from now on it would be a more measured form of self-indulgence; one balanced out by the knowledge that success takes a clear head and a lot of hard graft.

"I can drink, and I'm not going to say that I don't party," she explained. "But it's not every day, and it's no longer a tool for my creativity. I still drink and party but there's no darkness now, just a lot of fun."

She might no longer use alcohol or drugs as a tool for her creativity, but she got at least one song out of her druggy escapades: 'Beautiful, Dirty, Rich', written during this dark period in her life and one of the best-loved songs on her début album, *The Fame*. "I was doing a lot of drugs when I wrote 'Beautiful, Dirty, Rich'," she told *Rolling Stone*, revealing why she wrote it and what it was about. "It was about a few different things. First and foremost the record is about: whoever you are or where you live, you can self-proclaim this inner fame based on your personal style, and your opinions about art and the world, despite being conscious of it."

She continued: "It's also about how on the Lower East side, there were a lot of rich kids who did drugs and said that they were poor artists, so it's also a knock at that." She quoted the lyrics: "'Daddy, I'm so sorry, I'm so, so sorry, yes, we just like to party.' I used to hear my friends on the phone with their parents, asking for money before they would go buy drugs. So that was an interesting time for me, but it's funny that what came out of that record – because it's about many different things – ultimately what I want people to take from it is 'bang-bang'. That, no matter who you are and where you come from, you can feel beautiful and dirty-rich."

Chapter 5

Bands On The Run

"I didn't know what to do till I discovered Bowie and Queen."
— Lady Gaga

Like the first album by New York's Scissor Sisters, a record that really impressed Stefani Germanotta on its release in 2004, both because the band were fellow alumni of the city's underground club scene and because of the music's sheer diversity, Lady Gaga's *The Fame* was nothing if not eclectic. The range of styles on her début album was the upshot of a life spent listening to all sorts of music, and of an adolescence spent performing in bands of all musical types. The quality of these bands' output wasn't great, and the impression given is of a budding artist, confused by all the options available, casting around for a style to call her own. Nevertheless, her ceaseless search for the right environment for her ideas indicates a keen mind, one open to options and opportunities.

The chronology of all these pre-fame – or rather, pre-*The Fame* – outfits that she either formed or spent time in is a little hazy, but a straight reading of the credits on the fold-out booklet that accompanied *The Fame* CD would suggest that they were, in order, Mackin Pulsifer, SGBand and Lady Gaga & The Starlight Revue.

Mackin Pulsifer is very likely the name of the classic-rock covers band playing versions of Led Zeppelin, Pink Floyd and Jefferson Airplane songs that she formed while in her early teens (see Chapter 2). The Stefani Germanotta Band (otherwise known as the SGBand) was her next group of note if not merit, and reports indicate that the band lasted from September 2005 – just after she quit her studies at New York University – to the middle of 2006. They comprised Eli Silverman on guitar, Alex Beckman on drums, Calvin Pia on bass and, on vocals and keyboards, Stefani Germanotta herself.

Bassist Pia has spoken about the SGBand, and about how they used to rehearse in a "really dingy practice space" on New York's Lower East Side. It was apparently located beneath a grocery store, behind huge metal doors, through which Stefani would saunter with her keyboard, having wheeled the instrument down the street from her apartment at the intersection of Rivington and Suffolk.

By November 2005, the SGBand had begun working on a five-track demo known as the 'Words EP', with producer Joe Vulpis. It would be sold at the venue The Bitter End in January 2006 and included 'No Floods', an epic ballad that Gaga had previously performed live in the street on NBC's Channel 4 for the annual Columbus Day Parade in New York City on October 10, 2005. The programme's host, Maria Bartiromo, was suitably awestruck by the performance: "She's only 19," she gasped, "and what a voice."

By March 2006, there was another EP's worth of material – compositions by Germanotta, production by Vulpis – bearing the title 'Red And Blue', and it, too, was sold at The Bitter End. It included mainly big-voiced ballads with titles such as 'Something Crazy' (also known as 'When You're Not Around'), 'Wish You Were Here' and 'Red And Blue'. The songs featured a piano-heavy style that Lady Gaga later pursued, most obviously on the track 'Brown Eyes' from *The Fame*. Alongside these tentative early recordings came a series of live dates, where the SGBand road-tested the unreleased likes of 'Hollywood', 'Master Heartbreaker', 'John's Song', 'Walk The Road' and even a version of Led Zeppelin's 'D'Yer Mak'er'. You can see the SGBand performing the last-named track at The Bitter End on YouTube; preceding it by asking the small crowd, "Do you like reggae?", Germanotta is barely recognisable as the future Lady Gaga, with her long, straight brown hair and plain, drab vest. The only concession to the kind of glam flamboyance that we would later know and love her for was with her jeans, which she wore tucked into a pair of white boots.

The SGBand fell apart when several members began to find the twin demands of school work and gigging too much. Following the split, her bandmates never spoke to Stefani Germanotta again. In fact, the only time they would see her would be onstage or television, as Lady Gaga. Calvin Pia did try calling her once just as she began to make it big, but not surprisingly by then her phone number had been changed.

Within a few months Germanotta had teamed up with another Lady – Lady Starlight – to form The Starlight Revue, which would bring some of Stefani's burlesque experience and colour, and Starlight's fashion expertise, to bear on a 'group' that seemed to consist of the two girls cavorting about in very little clothing to heavy metal music. The two women would plot and scheme in Stefani's apartment about what they would do at their shows; there, they would customise their bikinis and listen to old David Bowie and New York Dolls records. "We thought, 'What could we do to make everybody so jealous?'" said Gaga, something of a

New York doll herself, later on. "We did it, and everybody was so jealous. And they still are."

The pair played gigs at downtown club venues such as The Mercury Lounge, The Bitter End and the Rockwood Music Hall. Central to the shows was a live performance art piece known as 'Lady Gaga & The Starlight Revue', while the concert itself was billed as 'The Ultimate Pop Burlesque Rockshow', their act a tribute to the early Seventies.

David Bowie was key in all this; Bowie and Queen. "I didn't know what to do till I discovered Bowie and Queen," she later told Adrian Thrills of *The Daily Mail*. Stefani had attempted a fusion of music and theatre before when she danced at burlesque clubs, but this was something different, something closer to glam and the theatricality of rock'n'roll. She told *Wound* magazine that, through Bowie, she began listening to theatrical metal bands such as Iron Maiden, who knew how to put on a colourful, dramatic show. "I started thinking about the theatrics of performance," she said. "That's when I really discovered myself."

Although she had not yet officially announced it to the world, it was around this time that Stefani Germanotta began to slowly shed her old skin and toy with the idea of being reborn as someone completely different, someone far removed from the nice middle-class Italian-American girl from Yonkers. She even suggested that, together with Lady Starlight, they should create a pop/metal hybrid, but that idea came to nought.

Still, at least she was trying things out, even if they were more grand follies at this point. Besides, eventually all of this madcap behaviour was bound to catch the right sort of attention, and it did when Stefani's various pop, rock, ballad and burlesque performances found the ear and eye of producer Rob Fusari. Originally from New Jersey, Fusari had worked with R&B superstars Destiny's Child (he co-wrote two of their biggest hits: 'No No No' and 'Bootylicious'), as well as Britney Spears and

The cat in the hat. (DAVID LEE/VISTALUX/REX FEATURES)

Stefani Germanotta before her transformation into Lady Gaga.

Still no sign of the avant-garde space-popster to come.

An early performance by Gaga as the conventional pop balladeer.

stefani live

@ sin-e
150 attorney st @ stanton
(b/t Houston and Stanton)
212.388.0077

April 13
8:00 pm

J M Z to Essex
F to 2nd ave or Delancey

Lady GaGa Please

Poster for Stefani live in New York.

Not your traditional festival fare: performing at Lollapalooza on August 4, 2007 in Grant Park, Chicago.

Lady Gaga performed a special 75 minute show at G.A.Y. in London on July 4, 2009, during which she changed her outfit on four occasions. (ROB CABLE/LFI)

Lady Gaga, New York, May 2008. (MICK ROCK/RETNA PICTURES)

On stage at the Oxford Arts Factory on September 24, 2008 in Sydney, Australia. 'Poker Face' had been released the day before in Australia. (DON ARNOLD/WIREIMAGE)

Who is that masked lady?: the V Festival at Hylands Park in Chelmsford, England on August 23, 2009.
(SAMIR HUSSEIN/GETTY IMAGES)

Radio station Z100's Jingle Ball, held at Madison Square Garden, New York on December 12, 2008.

(ELLA PELLEGRINI/NEWSPIX/REX FEATURES)

Jessica Simpson among many others – he was clearly used to pop divas.

According to the Gagapedia – the online encyclopaedia for all information on matters relating to Lady Gaga – the club entertainer was chosen by Bob Leone, National Projects Director of the celebrated Songwriters Hall of Fame, to be one of nine performers in the 2006 New Songwriters Showcase at the Cutting Room, a recording studio in New York. She decided to perform one of her compositions, 'Hollywood', and it happened to get noticed by Wendy Starland, a songwriting collaborator of Rob Fusari. She was there to look for a girl under 25 who could in theory become the lead singer of a group like The Strokes, a sort of female-fronted garage band. "He couldn't be there that night," recalls Starland of Fusari, "but he asked me to keep an eye out for somebody who had the ability and the desire, and that was definitely Stefani."

At the end of the set, Starland grabbed her and called Fusari at home. He was annoyed at being woken up so late, but his interest was piqued when she told him: "I may have found your girl."

Fusari reluctantly agreed to meet her. When Stefani finally arrived by bus at his office, he was initially disappointed. "I was hoping that wasn't her," he said, describing her as looking, "for want of a better term", like a 'guidette' – urban US slang for a highly sexualised and overtly sexily attired Italian-American, usually from New Jersey (a kind of Eastern Seaboard version of 'chav' or 'Essex girl'). "I had a clear vision of what she should look like and that wasn't it. I was hoping to find someone who looked a little grungy, like they just rolled out of bed."

The producer was intrigued by Stefani's appearance and the mix of styles that she used in her mode of dress – "quirky" was the word he used to describe it – but could see that it needed some work. "There was something very Sixties about her but also something sort of Nineties," he said. It was a similar story when it came to her music, whereby initial scepticism gave way to intrigue and then excitement. While talking to her, he found her page on PureVolume – the site for rising artists to host their MP3s – and played some of her songs in the background. He considered her material, all those over-the-top ballads, a bit "wedding band-ish", but his abiding impression was of a singer-songwriter with considerable promise, so he invited her down to his recording studio. Fusari asked her to sample one of her songs on the piano, so she played 'Hollywood'. Within seconds, he experienced an epiphany of sorts, and his mind was made up. It was a life-changing moment. So convinced was he of her potential that, while she was playing the song, he was on his BlackBerry, busy e-mailing his attorney. Recalls Fusari: "I was like, 'I need a contract tomorrow.' I totally saw superstar potential. I just didn't know in what form or what genre it was going to be."

Talking about the style of music Stefani was playing at this time, Fusari told *Billboard* magazine that "she had a big Gwen Stefani/No Doubt thing going on. Some Fiona Apple, some Beatles." But she was, stylistically speaking, far from the disco/club/pop girl she would become on *The Fame*. In fact, as the producer remembers it, she was pretty much resistant to the idea of change, claiming that she "kicked and screamed, 'No! No! I love what we're doing. We're not changing it.'"

Fusari, too, was into what he and Germanotta were doing at the time, although he acknowledged that "it wasn't going to be an easy sell". His suggestion was to try something completely different – to ditch the live drums and at least some of the guitars and, with the producer himself manning the drum machine, to start with a beat and aim for something more dancey. She wasn't convinced this was a good idea, as Fusari remembers it. "She's like, 'No way. I'm not doing it.'"

Fusari recalls the pivotal moment when everything changed. That was the day that he read an article in *The New York Times* about how difficult it is for women to succeed in the rock milieu – the area, broadly speaking, in which Stefani was then operating and in which she hoped to make her career. The article detailed the way in which Nelly Furtado swapped her original folk-rock approach, hooked up with super-producer Tim 'Timbaland' Mosley, and embraced dance music. "My antenna went up," said Fusari. "I said, 'Stef, take a look at this. I'm really an R&B guy. I never produced a rock record in my life. I don't know, you think maybe we should shift gears?'"

Finally, after much arm-twisting over lunch at their regular haunt, Chili's, Fusari managed to get his young charge to agree to pursue a different direction. And so, with the producer sitting at an MPC drum machine and Stefani knocking out a piano riff, they came up with 'Beautiful, Dirty, Rich'. As far as her music was concerned, things would never be the same again. Or as Fusari put it: "We never went back to the rock stuff."

Chapter 6

Def Con One

"I used to wait outside his office for hours, hoping he'd take meetings with me about my songs, but it never happened."

— Lady Gaga

The influence of David Bowie and Queen might have been, in Stefani Germanotta's mind, crucial in the development of her career, but her breakthrough tune bore traces of quite different musicians, particularly Prince and Madonna. 'Beautiful, Dirty, Rich' featured a hip hop breakbeat, synthesizers and a pounding dance rhythm that was far more in an urban/club/electronic funk vein than in any way connected with glam or anthemic rock – at a pinch, you could detect in the song certain elements of Eighties Bowie circa *Let's Dance*.

Lyrically, as detailed in Chapter 4, it concerned Germanotta's experiences as a struggling artist on New York's Lower East Side, when she was "doing a lot of drugs" and "trying to figure things out". The line, "Daddy, I'm so sorry, I'm so s-s-sorry, yeah," according to its author, was inspired by "rich kids" in the area whom she would hear calling their parents for money to buy drugs with, while the seediness and dangerous excitement of New York's nightlife, and its poor but up-for-it scenesters, was captured in the lines: "Our hair is perfect, while we're all getting shit-wrecked..." Later, on its release as an album track on *The Fame*, it got singled out by one reviewer as "a dizzying sonic trip that approximates the high point of a chemically enhanced night of club-hopping."

'Beautiful, Dirty, Rich' apparently started life as a rock song. During recording with producer Rob Fusari over at his 150 Studios in Parsippany-Troy Hills, New Jersey, Stefani was initially reluctant to add any programmed dance beats to the track, and the only thing that changed her mind was Fusari telling her that Queen used drum machines in their work. "I think that's what finally got her to give it a shot," he said.

She might have been resistant at first, but deep down she knew she had to try something if she was going to make it in the music business. She needed a new direction, both to keep audiences interested and herself entertained. Because even she was getting fed up with touting her pop-rock and piano-ballad wares at gigs around NYC. She said of one of her concerts, "I was like, 'If it wasn't me, I wouldn't listen to this. I would be bored at this show.'" She told *The Observer*: "It was like a baby becoming a toddler – at a certain point I smelled my own shit and I didn't like it."

The problem, she realised, was that she was just one of many, and that there was little about her musically at this point that stood out. When she began performing live in New York, when she was 14, just a girl with a piano and a clutch of songs, she was in the minority. Before long, however, as she saw it, "There were so many fucking songwriters. Everybody did the same shit, and it was super-boring. I wanted to do something that was original and fresh."

More and more, electronic pop music was looking like a viable way forward for her. She began to realise that pop was probably more "original and fresh", and more likely to provoke a positive response, than any so-called alternative music, especially in the underground circles in which she then mixed.

As though to support this theory, there was the night she was finally forced to accept that her old style of music wasn't cutting it any more and that major modifications were required. There she was, in a club, singing her songs, and nobody was paying any attention – and this despite her striking Amy Winehouse-style hair festooned with orchids ("I was a real flower child, but quite sweet with it") and the fact that she was wearing hot pants and a bikini top while setting fire to hairspray, as was her wont, underneath a disco mirrorball.

"There was this one night where I had a couple of drinks," she recounted to Fiona Sturges of *The Independent*. "I had new material and I had on this amazing outfit. So I sat down, cleared my throat and waited for everyone to go quiet. It was a bunch of frat kids from the West Village and I couldn't get them to shut up."

Her response to being ignored was dramatic, but there was no other option as far as she was concerned – "I didn't want to start singing while they were talking," she said. So right there and then, onstage in front of dozens, possibly hundreds, of inebriated college kids, she got undressed, right down to her bra and knickers, sat back down at her piano, and launched into her first song. Not surprisingly, the audience were now rapt.

This, she understood later, was the moment that Lady Gaga was born. It was also vindication of all the ideas about performance that the Andy Warhol acolyte had been harbouring and trying to put into practice for years. "That's when I made a real decision about the kind of pop artist that I wanted to be," she said. She felt that what she was doing was nothing less than performance art. "You can write about it now and it will sound ridiculous," she told a journalist, "but I was doing something radical."

All she needed now was a new name to go with her new

approach. One day in the recording studio with Rob Fusari, Stefani was singing her song 'Again Again' on the piano for her new producer when he apparently turned to her and said of her vocal style and general demeanour: "You are just so freakin' Freddie Mercury, you are so dramatic." This was meant as a compliment – being theatrical was a plus as far as Fusari was concerned, while Queen were one of his favourite bands, especially their hit 'Radio Ga Ga'. And so it was that, on arriving at the studio every day, instead of greeting her with a simple "hello", he would start singing 'Radio Ga Ga'. It became her entrance music.

But they still didn't have a stage name for Stefani, so they carried on coming up with suggestions. It was during one brainstorming session that she received a text from Fusari that read 'Lady Gaga'. It was a mistake, pure and simple. "It was actually a glitch," said Fusari. "I typed 'Radio Ga Ga' in a text and it did an autocorrect, so somehow 'Radio' got changed to 'Lady'." Stefani immediately texted him back. She loved it. From that day forwards, she was Lady Gaga, and nobody called her Stefani Germanotta again. Even her friends started to call her Gaga, with the 'Lady' prefix to add that all-important feminising touch, although apparently her mother continued to call her Joanne.

Lady Gaga wasn't the only new name Germanotta and Fusari came up with, because around this time they created the name Team Love Child for themselves. Actually TLC comprised Fusari, Gaga and her father, Joseph, and the name was registered in New Jersey as a domestic limited liability company. Basically, it was a production and writing company for the songs that Fusari and Gaga were writing together – most of them for Gaga, which she put on her MySpace or PureVolume sites, although some were for new artists such as Lelia Broussard and Lina Morgana – throughout 2006 and 2007. As for the name Team Love Child, it was chosen because Gaga liked to think of herself as "the hypothetical lovechild of David Bowie and Jerry Lee Lewis".

Of all the songs that TLC had been amassing, it was 'Beautiful, Dirty, Rich' that got the most attention when Gaga and Fusari began shopping around for a record deal. It was this song that led to her being signed, still aged 19, by Island Def Jam Music Group Chairman and CEO Antonio 'L. A.' Reid, although one report suggests that, ironically considering Def Jam was a hip hop/dance label, it was Gaga's older show-tune-style numbers that earned her the contract.

Whether it was the synthetic beat-driven side of her catalogue, the pop material or the more theatrical songs, somebody at Island Def Jam was impressed with the teenage singer-songwriter and her wide-ranging repertoire. Rob Fusari played Gaga's music to Joshua Sarubin, Vice-President of A&R at the label, and his response was simple: "I gotta get this girl in here next week," he is quoted as saying at nj.com. Sarubin's meeting with the newly christened Lady Gaga was memorable: "There was something unusual about her," he said. "She sat down at the piano in a showcase room and the way she played and the lyrics and the way she acted and sang was just so different and in your face, and you couldn't turn away. She was wearing these crazy white thigh-high boots and a black mini-dress and she had this presence like, 'I'm sexy and I don't care what anybody has to say about it.'"

It was during that fateful meeting on September 6, 2006 that chairman Reid dropped by to complain, good-humouredly, that he could hear the budding starlet all the way down the hall, in his office, so powerful was her singing voice. According to Gaga legend, he signed her on the spot to an artist development deal, with a first album scheduled for May 2007. If the music industry ever had a fairy tale, this was it.

Unfortunately, it didn't have a happy ending. Gaga complained that, after signing with Def Jam, she found it impossible to schedule a meeting with her boss, L.A. Reid, to discuss her work and the future direction of her career. "I used to wait outside his office for hours," she said, "hoping he'd take meetings with me about my songs, but it never happened."

Gaga was dropped after just three months as a Def Jam artist. "I was pretty devastated," she said, later admitting, "I know what it's like being on a label when they don't quite get it." Nobody could fathom the exact reason the company decided to sever her contract, but the fact was that, before the end of 2006, she was deal-less once more. Joshua Sarubin spoke about the situation later on, after Gaga had made inroads into the mainstream. "She maybe could have stayed with the label a little while longer," he explained, adding with the benefit of hindsight, "but I didn't want her to be in a situation where people didn't get it. She was too good. It was painful because I absolutely thought she was going to be my next big thing."

Gaga agreed that Def Jam failed to "get" her and feigned nonchalance whenever the subject came up. But as she explained to Adrian Thrills in *The Daily Mail*, with a rock'n'rolling dad who "followed in the footsteps of Bruce Springsteen", performing was in her bones and that, together with what she called her family's "ruthless work ethic", had made her into "a pretty fearless chick". Getting rejected was like water off a duck's back. "No matter how many times I was turned down," she said, "I kept coming back."

She wasn't always able to convey such resilience. "It was really hard," she confessed to *heat* magazine several years later about being dropped by Def Jam at such a young age, and after such a brief stint on the label. "I was 19. I'm 23 now. I did feel like I would die if I wasn't able to make music, because it was like everything was gone. The worst moment was when the label called me and told me I'd been dropped. I just cried. I lost it. I called my mum and she cried and said to me, 'I can't even put into words how much I know you're broken-hearted right now.' Someone said to me, 'You can't take it personally.' And I said, 'Fuck you. What's not personal about it? It's totally fucking personal.'"

Still, no matter how much her confidence was shaken by the Def Jam incident, there was really nothing that was going to stop her doing what she felt she was put on earth to do. And she owed her inner core of steel-tough strength to the city of her birth. As she declared: "I am New York. I'm a hustler. I ate dust since I was 15 and I kept going even when I was told 'no'."

Fortunately, there wouldn't be too many more 'no's' to come.

Chapter 7

Boys Boys Boys

"I like guys that listen to AC/DC and drink beers and buy me drinks just to show me off at the bar by the jukebox with their friends."

– Lady Gaga

Stefani Germanotta's rebirth as Lady Gaga has been seen as a triumph of feminist determination, and perhaps rightly so, but it didn't happen without the help of a series of powerful male industry figures: Rob Fusari, Vincent Herbert, Laurent Besencon, RedOne, Jimmy Iovine, Akon and Martin Kierszenbaum.

Producer Rob Fusari's contribution to her early career has been noted here and widely reported elsewhere (as was, in March 2010, his very public lawsuit against her over an alleged denial of royalty shares – see Chapter 20), but he wasn't the only one. It was Fusari who sent the songs that he had been writing with Gaga to another producer – and record executive – Vincent Herbert, who had helped create hits for the likes of Destiny's Child and Toni Braxton among many others. Herbert was so blown away by the Gaga/Fusari material that he lost no time in signing her to his brand new label, Streamline Records, set up as a subsidiary of Interscope Records.

Calling him the "industry love of my life", Gaga has credited Herbert as the man who discovered her, and compared and contrasted his treatment of her with that of Def Jam's L.A. Reid, who, as far as she was concerned, failed to divine her true potential before dropping her from his label. "He [Herbert] saw the artist I could become. He really helped develop and hone my skills by talking to me and introducing me to the right people." She would later say of him that, "I really feel like we made pop history, and we're gonna keep going."

It was Fusari, too, who hooked Gaga up with another key collaborator, Nadir Khayat, alias RedOne, the Moroccan-Swedish producer/songwriter whose credits include work for New Kids On The Block, Brandy, Robyn and Lionel Richie. Then there was Laurent Besencon who, as co-head of Gaga's own management company, New Heights Entertainment, could easily have let her go when Def Jam did, but stuck with her because he could see the heights she was capable of reaching. Besencon acknowledged her potential while also identifying that she needed a new sound for her new label and was instrumental in directing Gaga towards fellow New Heights artist RedOne, figuring that he might just be the one to tease it out.

In fact, it has been suggested that Gaga, disillusioned by the Def Jam affair, was wondering in the miserable aftermath whether she should give up music completely and pursue another career. Apparently, it was Fusari who encouraged her to take a break instead and spend time with her family while she pondered her future. And it was Besencon who ultimately made the Gaga-RedOne team-up happen, despite the latter's initial reluctance.

"My manager called me and said, 'You have to meet this girl – she is the most incredible artist,'" RedOne told a journalist. "If someone is good, it doesn't matter to me if that person has a deal. The first day we worked together, we came up with a song called 'Boys Boys Boys' and we just clicked."

'Boys Boys Boys' was inspired by two classics of trash-metal: Mötley Crüe's 'Girls, Girls, Girls' and AC/DC's 'T.N.T.'. It was in her exposition of the song and its genesis that Gaga revealed a lot about her worldview and character. "I wanted to write the female version of Mötley Crüe's 'Girls, Girls, Girls'," she explained, "but with my own twist. I wanted to write a pop song that rockers would like. I wrote it as a mating call." She added, by way of elucidation, that she was dating "this guy who was really into heavy metal and I wanted to write a pop song that would make him fall in love with me." She said that she went on to date him for the next two years, so clearly her compositions had some kind of aphrodisiacal effect. Moreover, the song, she said, had a subtext, which was as follows: "Even though I'm a very free and sexually empowered woman, I'm not a man-hater. I celebrate very American sentiments about bars and drinking and men buying women drinks. It's a very heavy metal sentiment that I celebrate in a pop song."

Gaga talked at length about the song 'Boys Boys Boys' and about her romantic, even antediluvian vision of male-female relations, in an interview with Laura Barton of *The Guardian*. She confirmed that, yes, she wrote it "to impress a guy", going on to reminisce about her first proper boyfriend – "the first love of my life", as she described him – who used to drive her around in a watermelon-green Chevrolet El Camino with a black hood. It was just the sort of car she always dreamed she'd be chauffeured around in, just as the boy was her dream lover.

The boy's name was Luke and he was the drummer in a heavy metal band. She adored him, the kind of adoration you see in a retro movie about Fifties high school romance: "I was his Sandy and he was my Danny," she said, referring to the John Travolta and Olivia Newton-John characters in the musical *Grease*. "He [had] long jet-black hair and [looked] like half-Neil Young, half-Nikki Sixx when they were young, and the way that he [talked] about his car and the way that he [stalled] the gas when he [turned]. . ." She sounded like a dizzy teenager swooning over the school hunk, rather than a ruthlessly determined pop star. "I like guys like that," she continued, getting quite carried away, "guys that listen to AC/DC and drink beers and buy me drinks just to show me off at the bar by the jukebox with their friends. That's kind of like an old hot groupie chick."

She confessed that this was the model for her new alter ego, one that was slowly (actually not that slowly) but surely taking shape: Gaga as the ultimate white trash accessory to the quintessential heavy metal bad-boy lifestyle. "I don't think a lot of female pop stars embrace womanhood in that domestic, American way," she said. "And me singing about gasoline and cars and beers and bars is very American."

The lyrics to 'Boys Boys Boys' bore out this idea that she was in love with a mythical notion of America, an America of cars and girls ("I lurrrrrve Springsteen," she said), one that hadn't changed much since the Fifties: "We like boys in cars/ Boys boys boys/Buy us drinks in bars," went the words to the song, which went on to fantasise about making out in the bleachers with a bequiffed rebel in denim who refers to the female protagonist as "legs". "It's like that sort of by-the-boardwalk mentality," she waxed lyrical to Laura Barton. "Girls either don't know about it or they think no one can relate to it or they think it's cooler to act like men and cheat on their boyfriends and yunno." She might have been a fast-rising role model for young females everywhere, but she wasn't about to turn her back completely on the old roles. She complained of women today: "They're, 'I don't want plastic surgery! Fuck plastic surgery! And fuck cooking you dinner! I'm gonna fucking order in!'" Gaga, she insisted, was different. She was just an old-fashioned girl. "I'm not like that – I used to make my boyfriend dinner in my stilettos, with my underwear on. And he used to be like, 'Baby, you're so sexy!' And I'd be like, 'Have some meatballs.'"

She confirmed her predilection for "wild boys" in an interview with *more!* Long hair, leather – these were, she said, a few of her favourite things. But she struck a poignant note when she admitted that romance with such untameable creatures ("I have a weakness for long hair, leather and a dark side," she said, offering by way of example notorious American goth-rocker Marilyn Manson) was usually doomed to failure. Besides, as she pointed out, contrary to appearances – and Lady Gaga was starting to earn a reputation for her extraordinary outfits – she wasn't really a wild child herself. "I'm not quite as outrageous as I look," she said. "Underneath all this I'm deeply moral and actually a really nice girl. I look so wild but I'm not. In the bedroom I like to wear pearls around my neck – I really am a lady."

Gaga wasn't quite prepared to submit completely to male will, however. This fantasy vision of modern life as some kind of *Happy Days*-style throwback, where the men are all Fonz lookalikes and the girls are grateful, was just that – a fantastical place to holiday briefly, but not actually live. When she was asked how she would respond were a boyfriend to make demands about her increasingly revealing outfits, she said she would "tell him to get lost – I never let a man tell me how to dress, how to look, how to perform. That's who I am and if they can't handle it then I'd rather be alone with my music. Nobody," she said grandly, "tells Gaga what to do!"

And nobody was going to get in the way of Gaga's path to global pop glory, no matter how closely they adhered to her conception of bad-boy perfection. Actually, his bad-boy credentials remain unknown, but there is another crucial male in the Lady Gaga firmament: Matthew Williams (sometimes known as Matty or Dada), one of the chief architects of her fashion team the Haus of Gaga and her principal creative director for many years. He is also one of Gaga's ex-boyfriends, but she called time on the relationship because it got in the way of their more important creative partnership.

"Dada is quite brilliant and we were crazy lovers," Gaga said, "but I stopped it when we discovered what a strong creative connection we had. I didn't want it just to be about careless love." If Gaga was going to be as big as she wanted to be, relationships with men – the non-professional variety – would have to take a back seat. As she told *Wound* magazine in December 2008: "I don't have a boyfriend. I'm married to my work. I don't really care about anything but my work." As she reasoned, her work, her beloved music, would never – as did her first love, Luke – wake up one day and tell her he didn't love her any more. Music would never let her down or break her heart.

All of this lay behind 'Boys Boys Boys' – seemingly an upbeat pop track with a simple, celebratory lyric. But then, that was Gaga all over – as shallow or as deep as you wanted her to be. There were layers of meaning if you wanted to find them, or you could react instantly to the pop fizz and buzz. When RedOne played the track to Akon, with whom he had a production company called RedOneKonvict, the R&B entertainer and entrepreneur in charge of urban pop label Kon Live Distribution was so impressed that he wanted Lady Gaga to be a writer for other artists on parent label Universal, such as Nicole Scherzinger of Pussycat Dolls, Fergie of The Black Eyed Peas and New Kids On The Block.

Talking about this period when she, the odd-looking, bizarrely dressed arty girl with the eccentric approach to song construction and lyric writing, was honing her chops, she said, "I was like the weird girl who dressed like a zoo animal, the trash glamour in a roomful of urban hip hop cats. They'd be like, 'Gaga, what do you think of this lyric?' and I'd twist it all up and all of a sudden it was edgy."

For Gaga this phase in her life was all about Men Men Men – men seemed to understand this extreme female, this caricature of womanhood, more instantly than women did. For example, there was Jimmy Iovine, the chairman of Interscope-Geffen Records, who told her, "I really get you" and secured a deal with Kon Live Distribution, a subsidiary of Universal Records. She also joined the roster of Cherrytree Records, another Interscope offshoot, this one formed to develop new talent. Cherrytree had been set up by producer and songwriter Martin Kierszenbaum – Gaga and Kierszenbaum would later write the songs 'Eh, Eh (Nothing Else I Can Say)', 'The Fame' and 'I Like It Rough' for her album *The Fame*.

The one high-profile female figure in this significant part of the Lady Gaga story was record company executive Jody Gerson, who got Gaga to ink a music publishing deal with Sony/ATV. This meant she would be available for hire to write songs for the likes of Britney Spears, a teenage idol of Gaga's, one who she used to follow around New York in a bid to catch a glimpse of her. Indeed, Gaga would later pen 'Quicksand', a bonus track for Britney's 2008 album *Circus*, about which she said, "There's something quite remarkable about writing a song when you're 20 and hearing a pop superstar sing it."

Gerson was delighted to be involved with Gaga at this exciting stage in her career. She told *Billboard* magazine that she knew Gaga would become not just an in-demand songwriter but a huge star in her own right. "She blew me away from the moment I met her," she said. "She was already signed to Interscope, and we are so lucky to all be on the same page and have a great working relationship."

It was Lady Gaga's relationship with another female – another Lady, in fact – that would prove essential in her journey to the top.

Chapter 8

A Wizard, A True Starlight

"Working with somebody that's better than you are, you become greater."

– Lady Gaga

Lady Gaga is nothing if not a total fan – of pop, and of pop people. As much as the kids who buy her records and scream at her concerts, she has her own idols and artists whom she adores. She's quite indiscriminate in her worship, though. Andy Warhol, David Bowie, Prince, Madonna and Chanel get singled out for special thanks on the foldout booklet that accompanies her début album, *The Fame*, the implication being that these would comprise the top five in any list of her all-time heroes and heroines. But that would be to ignore what she has said about, to name just one of her other passions, Grace Jones: "She is such an inspiration to me," she told website I'm Not Obsessed, explaining that she was drawn to Jones' androgynous appearance, particularly because of "all the rumours that have flown around over the years" about her own sexual make-up and orientation. She continued: "It's this kind of fascinating thing that nobody understands or wants to understand unless you're in the beautiful subculture that is my fans and the gay community." Speaking to *The Sun* in 2008 she was less florid but just as unswerving in her praise for the extraordinary Jamaican-American model, actress and funk diva. "Grace Jones is so amazing I vomited," she told Britain's biggest-selling daily newspaper.

Over the years, Gaga has been just as rapturous in her praise for acts as varied as Led Zeppelin, The Beatles, Elvis Presley, Pink Floyd, Bruce Springsteen, AC/DC, Guns N' Roses and Queen. Every one of these musicians or bands is the best, the ultimate, her favourite in the world, ever. But it's not just classic acts that she lionises. She has spoken often about how she idolised Britney Spears as a teenager, while at the Grammy Awards ceremony in 2009 *The Sun* reported that her father, Joseph, approached Britney at an after-show party to inform her that his daughter was "her biggest fan".

Then there is a relatively recent band like Scissor Sisters, about whom, on website About.com, Gaga came over all, well, gaga and gushed: "Oh, I love them, I can't breathe. I remember the first time I heard them, it was on the radio, and I was like, 'Who the heck is that?' They are a big influence. I love the disco, their outfits, and they really care about their performance. Conceptually I just think they're very smart in their approach. I'm also a big Elton John fan, and you can hear the influence on every record, so I love them. They were big – I really thought about them when I did 'Beautiful, Dirty, Rich'."

Gaga also maintains this level of fannish devotion for all the people she works with, the musical allies and industry insiders who have been instrumental in steering her career to date. Vincent Herbert, RedOne, Matty 'Dada' Williams, Jimmy Iovine, Akon, Rob Fusari – each of them has been singled out as the most important, the key player, the one without whom, etc, in her irresistible rise to the top (although the litigious Fusari appears less often on a Gaga pedestal these days – see Chapter 20). Rather than recoil at the suggestion that her collaborators have been essential to her career, she takes every opportunity to laud them to the hilt. "RedOne is like the heart and soul of my universe," she told About.com. "I met him and he completely, one hundred and fifty thousand percent wrapped his arms around my talent, and it was like we needed to work together. He has been a pioneer for the Haus of Gaga and his influence on me has been tremendous. I really couldn't have done it without him." As for Akon, he has been "a very talented songwriter to work with. His melodies, they're just insane. He keeps me on my feet, very grounded, but he also puts me on a silver platter, which is always very nice. So it's been an incredible influence."

Gaga's theory about teamwork goes like this: "Working with somebody that's better than you are, you become greater." She is the polar opposite of those stars who refuse to acknowledge antecedents or influences and want to give the impression that they arrived fully-formed without anything as undignified as a helping hand or a leg-up. She's also about as far removed as you can get from Grace Jones' icy hauteur – whenever the subject of one of her musical forebears or music business associates comes up, she's less disdainful dominatrix than giggly schoolgirl.

But Lady Gaga arguably reserves her most fulsome admiration for Lady Starlight, whom we last met in Chapter 5 as she joined Gaga for some burlesque dancing in New York's less salubrious dives. Gaga and Starlight went out as a duo, as Lady Gaga & The Starlight Revue. They also co-hosted a weekly party called New York Street Revival and Trash Dance in which they performed choreographed go-go dance routines to Seventies and Eighties hits, and generally cavorted about in outrageous costumes (tiny bikini tops, sequined knickers), utilising cans of hairspray that they set on fire so that they could shower the audience with sparks. "It was like a Seventies variety show," Gaga has said. "All the rock boys wanted to take us home for drinks."

Gaga has never been backwards in coming forwards to proclaim Lady Starlight – born Colleen Martin in December 1975 – one of the crucial characters in her story, and the one who encouraged her to make the transition from Stefani Germanotta to Lady Gaga, particularly with regard to her fashion sense. And neither has Starlight herself. "It was me who inspired her crazy style," said the philosophy graduate turned rock DJ, promoter and dancer who worked by day as a make-up professional for MAC Cosmetics and brought some glam-trash glamour to bear on New York clubland in the early Noughties. "My style, performance art and DJing inspired her persona. Now she's gone on to become a global phenomenon and I'm so proud."

Lady Starlight was a sort of latter-day, female Rodney Bingenheimer, that semi-legendary ligger-cum-mover-and-shaker on the Seventies LA scene – she even, from 2004 to 2006, ran something called Lady Starlight's English Disco, surely a nod to Bingenheimer's own English Disco that ran on the Sunset Strip in the early-to-mid-Seventies. The self-styled "rock'n'roll nightlife queen of downtown New York", her penchant was for the glitz and glitter of Bowie circa Ziggy Stardust and the spandex'n'leather of metal.

It was Starlight who nurtured Gaga's DIY sensibility and persuaded her to parade around onstage in skimpy PVC underwear and Indian headdresses. "The outfits were quite often stuck together with glue," said Starlight who, over a decade older than Gaga, ought to have known better. "Sometimes they held up and sometimes they fell apart onstage. We always wanted the flashiest garments possible... and to be as naked as possible." More seriously, she did exert an influence on Gaga with regard to presentation and image and provided the segue between her early DIY trash fashion look and the more sophisticated avant-couture designs she started to wear once the Haus Of Gaga had been built.

Starlight and Gaga first met on the latter's 20th birthday. They hit it off immediately. "We were both ladies," Lady Starlight said. "She put a dollar bill in my panties and the rest is history." This was before Gaga had begun her rise to fame, back when Starlight was "spinning heavy metal records at edgy Manhattan club St Jerome's and Gaga was dating one of her friends, Luc Carl", according to a *Daily Mirror* story about her headlined 'The Woman Who Invented Lady Gaga'. Later, when Lady Gaga's star was in the ascendant, Lady Starlight would insist that she didn't mind that she had been left behind, mainly because her influence on Gaga was evident for all to see and because Gaga herself wasn't afraid to say so.

"It's crazy knowing that the biggest star in the world was inspired by me," she has said. "But I was the one who told her to take her trousers off because I rarely wore any myself. She's always been so great on talking about me. Giving credit where it's due rarely happens in the music industry, but Gaga has always done that and I'm very grateful for that. As I'm 11 years older than Gaga, I do see myself as her mentor."

As time went on, Starlight and Gaga's NYC shows improved and as a result they received better and better reviews. Inevitably, word began to spread about this dynamic, colourful female duo. In August 2007, they were invited to Chicago, to perform at Lollapalooza, the prestigious rock festival and something of an alt-rock institution in the States. It was as intriguing a contrast of opposites as any in the annals of rock festivals, right up there with Laura Nyro's famously out-of-place appearance at Monterey in 1967, although mercifully the girls weren't treated anywhere near as badly as novelty pop duo Daphne & Celeste, who got bottled off stage during their performance at the Reading Festival in 2000.

In fact, although they were surrounded by rock bands such as Kings Of Leon and Yeah Yeah Yeahs, they were well received by the indie rock crowd. This is despite – or perhaps because of – Lady Gaga's outfit, which began as a sparkly blue dress, and then consisted, after stripping off, of black bikini briefs and matching black stockings, both featuring tiny mirrors as trim, and a shimmery silver bikini top that was entirely made out of not quite so miniature versions of these mirrors.

There is footage of Gaga and Starlight, the latter in a yellow bikini, on YouTube performing a song at Lollapalooza called 'Blueberry Kisses', which, to say the least, contrasts strikingly with traditional festival fare – it sounds like something from a Seventies rock'n'soul revue, and is barely recognisable as the work of today's Gaga, that ultra-modern purveyor of sci-fi techno-disco. That said, her vocals are as powerful as ever. Indeed, her voice, belting out the song to reach the festival-goers way out in the crowd, is strangely reminiscent of Amy Winehouse's. Ironically, throughout her time at Lollapalooza, revellers would shout out "Amy! Amy!" as Gaga walked by, but it was probably no surprise, really, considering that Winehouse – another twentysomething female with strong features, long, dark hair and tattoos – was also performing at Lollapalooza that weekend.

Notwithstanding their unusual attire and performance given the context, Gaga and Starlight's show was well received by the public and online commentators, who appreciated the way they imported a bit of New York clubland to the open-air festival milieu, complete with their trademark hairspray pyrotechnics, and the girls themselves enjoyed the show. "It was a blast," said Gaga, who told About.com that they just about overcame their nerves and the various technical problems they faced onstage. For Gaga, the best thing about Lollapalooza was "the sea of hippies and so forth that were there and not expecting what they saw"

– and what they saw, according to Gaga, was nothing less than "shock art".

However, probably most shocking of all that weekend at Lollapalooza was that Lady Gaga got a citation for indecent exposure for walking about the festival site in nothing but her tiny hot pants over spandex leggings and knee-high boots. She couldn't believe it – there, amid all the drug-taking long-hairs, she was singled out for her vaguely outré outfit.

"It's a music festival," she complained. "Everyone was doing drugs. And they arrested me for wearing hot pants? It was ridiculous."

Ridiculous, perhaps, but the whole Lollapalooza experience – paparazzi confusion with La Winehouse, controversy leading to a bust over her attire, and the appreciation of her music and ideas for presentation by a wider audience than any she had been exposed to to date – gave her a sense of the direction in which she was heading, even if it would be without Lady Starlight.

Chapter 9

From New York To LA

"You gotta have the fame, you gotta exude that thing. You gotta know and believe how important you are. You gotta have conviction in your ideas."

– Lady Gaga

Being the eccentric individual that she is, Lady Gaga took a slight detour on the road to fame. In November 2006 she bizarrely chose to become involved in the world of children's literature, in marked contrast to her most obvious antecedent Madonna, who didn't write her first kids' book until well into her music career. Still, there she was, featured on a couple of songs on the CD designed to accompany the book *The Portal In The Park*, the tale of an 11-year-old boy and his magical creature friends by the improbably named writer Cricket Casey. Even stranger was that her co-star on the two tracks, 'World Family Tree' and 'The Fountain of Truth', was original rapper Grandmaster Melle Mel. Gaga wrote 'The Fountain of Truth' herself, but insisted on changing her name on the credits from Stefani Germanotta to

Lady Gaga. She could obviously sense that the tide was turning in her favour and that changes were coming.

Lady Gaga has declared that she has felt famous her whole life, emphasising the difference between "famous" as in special, different, unique, a sort of local notoriety, and the sort of fame that means you're recognised all over the world. "Some people are just born stars," she once said. "You either have it or you haven't, and I was definitely born one. Even as a kid I always had eyes on me, like bees on honey. I was always outrageous and I was always very smart."

Fame, she furthered in *The Guardian*, is a state of mind, not a measure of the contents of your bank account. You can, she explained, feel "beautiful and dirty and rich", as her song went, almost by a process of visualisation and sheer will power, by simply feeling that you are, indeed, great. "Fame is not pretending to be rich, it's carrying yourself in a way that exudes confidence and passion for music or art or fishing or whatever the hell it is that you're passionate about, and projecting yourself in a way that people say, 'Who the fuck is that?'" She stressed that it wasn't a matter of money – she could, she argued, convey a sense of her "famousness" simply by wearing a $2 pair of trousers, a T-shirt and a cheap pair of sunglasses; by doing so she could easily give the impression that she was, in fact, as famous as her former schoolmate Paris Hilton. All you needed, she decided, was this precious commodity, this inner self-belief, called "the fame". "You gotta have the fame," she said, "you gotta exude that thing. You gotta make people care, you gotta know and believe how important you are. You gotta have conviction in your ideas."

True enough, from way back when she was just plain old Stefani Germanotta in high school, she was grabbing attention and causing a stir wherever she went, for the way that she dressed and the things that she said – she had the fame all right. And now as Lady Gaga she was enjoying a more widespread fame, or rather infamy, for much the same reasons. But she had yet to achieve renown on the scale that she had in mind, the sort of global celebrity enjoyed by her heroes listed in the last chapter. She had been through the "shock performance installation piece" phase of her career, she'd dabbled on the fringes with glam, metal and rock'n'roll, and experimented with a DIY version of art-trash fashion, but now she needed to do it on a bigger scale; she needed to find a vehicle that would carry her right into the mainstream. Whatever that vehicle was, it was becoming more and more evident that she wasn't going to find it in New York. Now, nobody loved New York more than Lady Gaga, and she was without doubt a quintessential New York doll, every bit as imbued with the essence of Manhattan as, say, Madonna or Carrie Bradshaw in *Sex And The City*. She loved all the art galleries and house parties, every sleazy club and back-alley dive bar, and all the neon-lit streets that she'd pounded in a bid to further her career and realise her ideas about "the fame".

She has affirmed how she favours the "old-fashioned/grass roots" path to success on her website, where she effectively pays tribute to her own ruthlessly self-disciplined rise to prominence on the streets of her beloved home town – by "paying her dues with seedy club gigs and self-promotion". The website commentary, which reads like a declaration of intent, goes on to make the distinction between Lady Gaga and her *American Idol* wannabe peers and their ilk. "This is one rising pop star who hasn't been plucked from a model casting call, born into a famous family, won a reality TV singing contest or emerged from a teen cable TV sitcom. I did this the way you are supposed to," Gaga proclaims on www.ladygaga.com. "I played every club in New York City and I bombed in every club and then killed it in every club and I found myself as an artist. I learned how to survive as an artist, get real, and how to fail and then figure out who I was as a singer and performer. And I worked hard."

And it was New York City that provided her with the necessary inspiration – in a way, it was her muse. She loved the street fashions and its geographical location, the way you could travel from there to anywhere in the world; she even loved, as she put it, "the coldness of the concrete". And she loved the urgency of the place, the speed of life there. Still, now that she was signed to Interscope, a label based in Santa Monica, California, it made sense for her to move out of New York, right across to the other side of the States, to Los Angeles.

She was reluctant to do so, and immediately seized the opportunity to slam the perceived pretentious lifestyle of Los Angelinos. "What am I supposed to do, canoodle with celebrities at a nightclub, with a lemon-drop Midori in my hand?" she wondered. "It's not the same as being in a bar that smells like urine with all your really smart New York friends."

She said goodbye to those smart New Yorkers on New Year's Eve 2007 when Gaga, Lady Starlight and their friend Darian Darling went out to celebrate at a farewell party in a bar on one of her favourite walkways, Rivington Street. It was, by all accounts, a wild affair, so much so that Gaga, who had turned up at the bar with all her luggage ready for the trip to LA the next day, lost her keys and mobile phone and spent most of the night carousing with her shirt off. When the taxi finally arrived at the bar in the early hours of the following morning to take her to the airport, Gaga was hung over and considerably the worse for wear, but she knew deep down that she was doing the right thing.

So she had changed address. To go with it, she needed a change of musical direction. And the direction she chose to go in was pop, the electronic variety. "I thought, 'If I wanna be really revolutionary, I'll make pop music.'" Pop, as she saw it, was more radical than the most alternative underground sounds. And her view was that it had become a forgotten art and needed someone with her intelligence and imagination to revive it, and give it a new lease of credibility.

Of course, with Gaga, nothing is ever simple, and her conception of pop was odd to say the least. She recited a list of some of her favourite 'pop' songs in *The Observer*. Led Zeppelin's 'Whole Lotta Love', The Beatles' 'Oh! Darling', Wilson Phillips' 'Hold On', AC/DC's 'TNT' and David Bowie's 'Rebel Rebel'. Even affording the term as broad a definition as possible, it is hard to see much pop there – hard rock, heavy metal, glam, MOR and doo wop pastiches, yes, but not much pop. Was this the sort of 'pop' Lady Gaga had in mind? No wonder she once said, "I think most music is pop music."

She had already proved herself as a songwriting gun-for-hire. When she was still a teenager back in New York she had been an intern at Famous Music Publishing, where she learned some of the tricks of the trade even as she turned up for work – much to the delight or despair, depending on who you asked, of her colleagues – in her underwear.

And when Famous Music was acquired by Sony/ATV Music Publishing, she struck a music publishing deal and wrote songs for Britney Spears (two were picked and recorded, but only one was released: 'Quicksand', a bonus track on European versions of Spears' *Circus* CD), on the back of which she was then commissioned to write, under the guidance of R&B stalwarts Akon and Rodney Jerkins, for Interscope labelmates New Kids On The Block, Fergie and Pussycat Dolls.

Akon had recognised her abilities while she sang a reference vocal for one of his tracks in the studio. "When we were working, Akon would say, 'Get in the booth and cut these vocals', and he'd always tell me I could really sing," she said. "So he decided he wanted to be a part of my music." The R&B whizz admired her work ethic and eclectic approach. "I think she's a magnet to the industry in general," he said, imagining that she could write songs that would appeal to pop audiences, dance cognoscenti and the hip hop community. He was thoroughly impressed: "She's brave. She's fresh. She's different. She's bold. She don't give a damn. You gotta take her as she is. That's the beauty of it. You're forced to like her the way she is without no extra stuff added." She was also a bundle of fun to work with. "She's like a sister to me," he said. "That's like my girl. She's right here, in a headlock!"

It was a fairly unusual move – to make it as a songwriter before diving headlong into the fray as a solo pop performer. An article in *The Scotsman* assessed Lady Gaga's chances of making that all-important transition from behind-the-scenes tunesmith to fully-fledged pop starlet. "Songwriters-turned-singers are in the minority," ran the article, "yet it's rare to find a female songwriter who is not penning lyrics in the hope of singing them herself." It cited as examples of songwriters turned successful artistes Dolly Parton, who boasts a catalogue of 600 songs and of course is a world-famous singer, too; and R&B singer Christina Milian, who first found success when, aged 19, she co-wrote the song 'Play' for Jennifer Lopez, and a recording contract followed soon afterwards.

The Scotsman also noted those females who had taken the reverse route, such as former 4 Non Blondes member Linda Perry, who became an incredibly successful and prolific songwriter for the likes of Gwen Stefani, James Blunt and Pink, and Nineties pop star turned songwriter-for-hire Cathy Dennis, who wrote, among others, Britney Spears' 'Toxic' and Kylie Minogue's 'Can't Get You Out Of My Head', two of the best pop songs of the Noughties. In Lady Gaga's opinion, it was not inconceivable to combine the two roles. "I want the imagery to be so strong that fans will want to eat and taste and lick every part," she said, somewhat obliquely. She added that she didn't want to be written off merely as a songwriter, and went on to sum up what, for her, made for a great pop song. "The mark of a great song is how many genres it can embody. It's about honesty and connection – look at a song like 'I Will Always Love You'. Whitney killed it as a pop song, but it works as a country song, a gospel song, everything. If I can play a song acoustic, or just on the piano, and it still works, I know it's good."

So much for her theorising and conjecture. Could she walk it like she talked it and write a perfect pop song?

Chapter 10

Pop Life

"Everyone is looking for a song that really speaks to the joy in our souls and in our hearts and having a good time. It's just one of those records."

– Lady Gaga

As though to prove that the best pop songs are more of a happy accident than the result of careful strategising, Lady Gaga wrote her first hit single in 10 minutes flat while suffering from the effects of alcohol.

It was January 2008 and Gaga had barely had time to recover from her flight to LA from New York, where she had had her farewell drink-up, when she met up with Akon and producer RedOne at The Record Plant in Los Angeles. This was the legendary recording studio where Fleetwood Mac recorded their masterpiece of MOR pop *Rumours*, The Isley Brothers created their soul-rock landmark *3+3* and where, more recently, Kanye West produced his modern rap classic *Late Registration*. She was overcome with excitement at being in the studio with its "very pristine, big huge room with giant speakers" and incredible history.

Later that month she would write songs, again with Akon, for Tami Chynn, an artist signed to Konvict Muzik in Atlanta, and she would also collaborate with Space Cowboy, the French-born DJ, record producer and musician known to his mum as Nick Dresti, who had worked with everyone from Paul McCartney to The Darkness. It was Martin Kierszenbaum (see Chapter 7) who introduced Space Cowboy to Gaga and the two hit it off instantly. The producer, who up to that point was the one with the track record, was immediately impressed by his new cohort.

"Nobody knew who she was, she was just starting up, and we spoke on the phone, we got on really, really well – it was amazing!" he said, captivated by her excitable chatter about David Bowie and Prince, disco balls and body paint. "We figured out that we shared pretty much the same experiences; we'd been doing similar things on opposite sides of the Atlantic. Then I got invited to the studio to write some songs with her: we did one called 'Starstruck' and another one called 'Christmas Tree'. She's super-creative, she's amazing – the best writer I'd ever seen, and best performer."

But it was the song that she put together in record time at The Record Plant with Akon and RedOne that would prove the most significant out of this early spurt of creativity. It was called 'Just Dance' and it was written with the express intention of creating, revealed Gaga, "a happy record".

Job done – albeit with caveats. 'Just Dance' was upbeat and captured well enough a sense of euphoria, only it was tempered by the knowledge that this was about the edgy joy one experiences while out of one's gourd on alcohol. It began with a machine beat from an Apple MacBook and a lyric, seemingly made up on the spot, that went, "I've had a little bit too much" – Gaga wanted it to be a song about being drunk, which made sense given the circumstances in which it was written. Soon she came up with more words plucked straight from her life, including references to the keys and mobile phone that she lost on that hedonistic last night in New York (see Chapter 9).

She explained the genesis of the song to *HX Magazine*: "I was taken very quickly out of my party lifestyle. I wrote it instantly – like it flew out of my body." She went on to discuss the meaning of lyrics such as, "I love this record, baby, but I can't see straight any more" and its allusions to being inebriated and disorientated on the dance floor ("Keep it cool, what's the name of this club?"). "If you've ever been so high that it's, like, scary, the only way you can deal with it is not deal with it, so you just kind of dance through the intoxication."

RedOne was evidently a key collaborator on the track because there is a 'shout-out' to the producer at the start (which has been misinterpreted as "red wine", a favourite tipple of Gaga's), as well as one to Gaga herself, which has become something of a signature component of her songs (see also her 2009 hit 'Bad Romance' and its strange, robotic refrain of "Gaga, ooh la la"). Now all that was required was audible proof of the presence of Akon, which duly came after he heard the finished track – he was so impressed by it that he added a verse, which was sung on the final version by Colby O'Donis, a young pop/R&B performer. Cue his own shout-out – to his record label, Konvict – during the intro.

As for the music, it seemed to reflect the lyrical content with its pounding rhythm replicating the delirious pleasure of dancing while sozzled, of dancing your distractions away. Anticipating any success she might enjoy with the song, Gaga suggested that 'Just Dance' might appeal, even provide comfort, chiming as it did with the times and the miserable lives people were leading beneath the shadow of the global credit crisis. "Maybe," she wondered, "the record will be appreciated more now there are lots of people who are going through rough times, losing jobs and homes."

The song details a night out on Planet Gaga, and finds our heroine trashed out of her skull and blind to anything but the pursuit of reckless thrills. As the electronic rhythm grinds on relentlessly and the ravey synths add a touch of menace, balanced out by sweetening girl-group "doo-doop"s from Gaga, Colby O'Donis joins her on the dance floor, admiring her moves and suggesting they go home together. As the song proceeds the delirium intensifies and the lyrics get weirder, offering a sense of intoxicated disorientation: "Half psychotic sick hypnotic". In a way, the lyrics serve as an oblique statement of intent from Lady Gaga about her decision to pursue a highly produced, grandiose electronic pop direction.

As she revealed to the Artist Direct website, 'Just Dance' may have been a document of a night of fleeting pleasure but it was the result of a lot of hard graft in the studio; furthermore, she said, not everyone who heard it ahead of its release believed in it or imagined that it would ever become successful. But that didn't matter for the moment because Gaga was delighted with it, seeing it as an example of pure songwriterly self-expression. 'Just Dance' realised perfectly her intention to make feel-good music that simultaneously satisfied her artistic impulses and sounded like the sort of accessible, commercial pop music that would connect with a large audience.

"I definitely follow my heart," she said, "but I would say the catalyst for making music and all art is to make something that's beautiful. I've always believed that art is beauty, and beauty is art. I wanted to make a beautiful record. I think 'Just Dance' is." She added: "Everyone is looking for a song that really speaks to the joy in our souls and in our hearts and having a good time. It's just one of those records. It feels really good, and when you listen to it, it makes you feel good inside. It's as simple as that. I don't think it's rocket science when it comes to the heart. I think it's a heart theme song."

So much for her opinion – what did everyone else think of it? Lady Gaga's début single received generally positive reviews. Matthew Chisling of Allmusic described it as "galactic", perhaps alluding to its sci-fi, cyber-pop feel or out-of-this-world atmosphere. Alexis Petridis of *The Guardian* called it a "beguilingly compulsive tale of pulling a drug-induced whitey, with a combination of clipped marching beats, sawing electronics and mild R&B flavour that bears a vague resemblance to Nelly Furtado's 'Maneater'." Ben Norman of About.com got quite carried away, likening the intro to "a Valkyrie leading the charge [and] riding triumphant ahead of her army."

Some reviewers noted that 'Just Dance' wasn't quite as radical a departure from pop music past as Lady Gaga might have imagined, comparing it to previous releases by Rihanna, Chris Brown and Pussycat Dolls, while others, focusing on the lyrics, considered it tame where Gaga probably intended it to induce shock and awe. One dismissed it as "bland dance fodder". However, most writers decided it was catchy enough for mainstream consumption and praised Gaga's strong vocal performance. "You won't get many more catchy party odes than 'Just Dance' this year, a polished gem set to lodge in your head for the next few weeks," commented Ben Hogwood of MusicOMH.com.

A few of the articles were ambiguous, highlighting the "mindlessly frothy synthpop that matches low-grade dance grooves with Gaga's icy, almost disembodied vocals about dancing bliss". People were finding it hard to pigeonhole 'Just Dance'. It was an irresistible club banger, it was sheer R&B deluxe, it was pure pop... One writer, perhaps subconsciously divining some similarity with David Bowie's equally pounding worldwide 1983 hit, mistakenly referred to it as 'Let's Dance'.

Most interesting of all were the writers who considered 'Just Dance' to be part of a global movement, a resurgence of the synthpop sound of the early-Eighties, led by a slew of solo female artists from around the world whose names all happened to start with the letter 'L': La Roux and Little Boots in Britain and New Zealand's Ladyhawke. *The Guardian* even ran a big feature on this brave new era of girl-dominated cyber dance music entitled 'Slaves to Synth', which featured the aforementioned Ls belles and declared: "The male guitar band is dead. The future is electro, female, DIY – and in your face." Interviewed for the article, Lady Gaga proclaimed, "There's a big empty space waiting to be filled by women."

As a largely electronic dance track, 'Just Dance' was remixed several times, each with different rhythms and textures and aimed at niche clubs, from trance to house to techno, with various added dub space, blips and beeps depending on which one you bought. It was also accompanied by a video, an inevitability for any artist let alone one as visually aware as Lady Gaga. The promo for her first single was directed by Melina Matsoukas, whose CV included videos for Kylie Minogue, Jennifer Lopez and Snoop Dogg, so clearly the expectation over at Interscope was that Lady Gaga would soon join this select pantheon.

The storyline, such as it was, involved a party scene – it begins with Gaga arriving with her dancers, Dina and Pepper, at a house party, which appears to have run its course due to the human debris and general air of debauchery and dishevellment. Gaga is filmed variously fingering a synth, dancing in a poncho or with a disco ball, and cavorting in a small rubber pool with an inflatable killer whale. She has beneath her right eye a blue, lightning bolt-shaped sticker, reminiscent of her idol David Bowie's *Aladdin Sane* lightning flash. Colby O'Donis makes a guest appearance as the babe magnet, and there are cameos from Akon and Space Cowboy.

In an interview with Australian radio in September 2008, Gaga explained: "The whole video is performance art about being drunk at a party," while to About.com she said of her virgin experience at a video shoot: "Oh, it was so fun, it was amazing. For me it was like being on a Martin Scorsese set. I've been so low budget for so long, and to have this incredibly amazing video was really very humbling. It was really fun, but you'll see if you ever come to a video shoot of mine one day – I'm very private about those things; I don't really talk to everybody. I'm not like the party girl running around. I might even seem to be a bit of a diva. I'm sort of with myself, in my work head-space worrying about costumes, and if extras look right, and placement. I don't just show up for things, you know. That video was a vision of mine. It was Melina the director who wanted to do something, to have a performance art aspect that was so pop but it was still commercial, but that felt like lifestyle. It was all those things, I love it."

With the video in place and all the various remixes and single formats on offer, all that remained now was to find out whether 'Just Dance' was merely pop on paper, or if it would actually prove popular...

Chapter 11

So Happy I Could Die

"'My fans in the UK are so sexy and the people are so innovative and free in how they think about pop culture and music. I was in my apartment in Los Angeles getting ready to go to dance rehearsal when they called and told me [about 'Just Dance' reaching number one], and I just cried."

– Lady Gaga

Talk about famous last words. Decca turning down The Beatles was one thing; this was a whole other level of misjudgement. Because, as Lady Gaga remembers it, there were some people at her record company who took one listen to 'Just Dance' and deemed it quite unsuitable for release.

"They would say, 'This is too racy, too dance-oriented, too underground. It's not marketable,'" she told *The Independent*. Luckily she had her response to the naysayers ready. "I would say, 'My name is Lady Gaga, I've been on the music scene for years, and I'm telling you, this is what's next.'"

She did, however, concede that, compared to a recent huge

Billboard's Fourth Annual Women In Music event at The Pierre Hotel on October 2, 2009 in New York City, where Debbie Harry was presented with the Icon Award. (JEMAL COUNTESS/GETTY IMAGES)

Performing at The GRAMMY Celebration Concert Tour at House of Blues in Boston, MA on May 4, 2009. Bubbles also featured in her *Rolling Stone* cover appearance that same month. (CHRIS POLK/FILMMAGIC)

Onstage at the launch of VEVO on December 8, 2009 in New York City, wearing a dress by Valentino. (THEO WARGO/GETTY IMAGES FOR VEVO)

The Museum of Contemporary Art's 30th Anniversary Gala in Los Angeles, November 14, 2009. (AP PHOTO/DAN STEINBERG)

"In the music industry there's still a tremendous amount of accommodation of homophobia, so I'm taking a stand."
Attending the National Equality March on October 11, 2009 in Washington, DC. (BRUCE GLIKAS/FILMMAGIC)

(AP PHOTO/ARIEL SCHALIT)

T in the Park Festival, Balado Scotland on July 11, 2009, which was headlined by The Killers. (SIMONE CECCHETTI/CORBIS)

Capital FM's Jingle Bell Ball at the O2 Arena in London, where she headlined over performers like JLS and Miley Cyrus. (SUZAN/EMPICS ENTERTAINMENT)

Lady Gaga with celebrity friends (clockwise): Dr. Dre (JOHN SHEARER/WIREIMAGE FOR BEST BUY), Elton John (KEVIN MAZUR/ WIREIMAGE), Perez Hilton (JERRITT CLARK/WIREIMAGE) and Madonna (DIMITRIOS KAMBOURIS/WIREIMAGE FOR MARC JACOBS).

Lady Gaga meets Kermit the Frog at the MTV Video Music Awards, Radio City Music Hall, on September 13, 2009.
(KEVIN MAZUR/WIREIMAGE)

The Kermit the Frog outfit, created by designer Jean Charles de Castelbajac, was apparently 'a commentary on wearing fur'. It was worn for a German TV interview.

(MICHAEL WILFLING/CONTOUR BY GETTY IMAGES)

worldwide hit single like Katy Perry's 'I Kissed A Girl', 'Just Dance' probably wasn't the sort of song that would automatically appeal to radio station programmers, while the genre she imagined it belonged to – electro-pop – was regarded as "dirty underground music", at least in the States.

It seemed at first as though those record company sceptics had a point. In America, 'Just Dance' was released three months after it was recorded, on April 8, 2008, and initially radio stations were reluctant to play it. So Lady Gaga, and the single, had to take the circuitous route to success. To start with, she performed the song on numerous television programmes in the US. She appeared on all the main American talk shows – for example, *Jimmy Kimmel Live* and *The Tonight Show With Jay Leno* – as well as reality TV contest *So You Think You Can Dance*. She was also on *The Ellen DeGeneres Show* where, ahead of her performance of the single, she sat on the former sitcom queen turned chat-show host's sofa for a brief interview, dressed in the most peculiar outfit: a futuristic leather jumpsuit slashed open down the front to reveal some of her breasts and most of her midriff, and a head-piece that resembled a gyroscope. It made greeting and embracing the TV host a little tricky. "It's a Gaga barrier," she and Ellen agreed, laughing. After a few minutes of friendly banter, the singer couldn't control herself any longer. She turned to DeGeneres, who famously "came out" at the height of her sitcom fame, and gushed: "I love you so much!" to huge cheers from the studio audience. DeGeneres took Gaga's hand as the Lady continued: "It means more to me to be on this show than anywhere. I look up to you so much, so thank you for having me." The crowd cheered and clapped. Ellen seemed genuinely flattered by Gaga's kind words. "Yeah, I heard you said something nice about me in an article," she responded as the mutual on-air love-fest continued, "and I appreciate it – I don't know what you said..." Her voice trailed off, so Gaga explained that she'd told an interviewer that she, DeGeneres, was an inspiration – "for women and the gay community". She was overcome. "I thought I liked you before," she told Gaga. "Now I like you more."

The TV campaign to make up for the lack of radio play for 'Just Dance' continued. In July, Gaga performed the single in front of more than a billion viewers worldwide during the swimsuit section of the Miss Universe 2008 beauty pageant in Vietnam. It was quite a show of contrasts – the conventionally pulchritudinous contestants and the alien she-creature in the outré couture. In Australia, Gaga performed the song on *Sunrise* and, not for the last time, her performance caused controversy – not, on this occasion, because of anything she wore or said, but because of allegations that she was lip-synching. Gaga denied this, aware of the censure of stars who fail to sing live, such as Milli Vanilli (whose career was famously derailed by a miming fiasco, ending in the suicide of one of the duo). She immediately issued a statement, in the wake of internet criticism by furious bloggers, which said: "I was sick the day of the show but I absolutely, 100 per cent, was singing live. I have never lip-synched and never will. Even on my worst day, I never will."

If radio was slow in responding to 'Just Dance', TV programmers were all over it like a cyber-pop rash – according to Jody Gerson, the woman who had signed Lady Gaga to Sony/ATV Publishing (see Chapter 7), by the summer of 2009 songs from Gaga's début album, *The Fame*, had been placed in TV shows (and films) over 100 times. 'Just Dance' was the most requested track, slightly ahead of 'Poker Face' (the next number to be lifted from the album for single release) and the title song. In fact, if there was a chart that measured a track's popularity with TV stations, 'Just Dance' would have been at the top of it.

'Just Dance' was also popular in the clubs ahead of its appearance in the regular charts (it also appeared on the Hot R&B/Hip-Hop Songs chart, where it peaked at 72), which also helped its slow infiltration of the mainstream. In the US, it was a real 'sleeper' hit, spending almost five months on the Billboard Hot 100 before finally reaching pole position in January 2009. It took 22 weeks to hit the top spot, the second-longest climb to number one since Creed's 'With Arms Wide Open' took 27 weeks to reach the summit in November 2000. (The single also broke another US record, a bizarre one: it was apparently the first song to hit the top spot on the US Hot 100 to include the word 'dance' since February 1991, when C + C Music Factory's 'Gonna Make You Sweat [Everybody Dance Now]' ascended to number one!)

Six months before that, in summer 2008, it had peaked at number two on both the Hot Dance Airplay and Hot Dance Club Play charts, proof of its popularity with hardcore clubbers ahead of its acceptance by pop fans. 'Just Dance' finally entered the Billboard Hot 100 chart at number 76 on August 16, 2008. Following its slow, inexorable rise, by January 2009 it was at number two and in one week alone that month sold 419,000 in downloads – making it the third-biggest single-week sum of all time; it went on to become the second-bestselling digital song of all time. Eventually, it rose to number one on the Pop 100 and, within a week, it was at number one on the Hot 100, too.

'Just Dance' topped the charts in the United States (where it earned the singer a Grammy nomination), Australia, Canada, the Republic of Ireland, the Netherlands and the United Kingdom, and reached the Top 10 in several other European countries, including Austria, Denmark, Finland, Norway, Sweden and Switzerland, as well as the Top 20 in Belgium and France. By March 2009, it had been certified three-times platinum by the Recording Industry Association of America (RIAA) for net sales of three million and had sold over five million downloads in the US, becoming only the second song to reach the five million mark in paid downloads. Its eventual worldwide sales tally would be in excess of eight million.

Australia took to 'Just Dance' before America did. The track débuted at number 34 on the ARIA (Australian Recording Industry Association) singles chart in July 2008, and moved up to 17 the following week. In September it topped the chart for one week before being replaced by Pink's single 'So What'. It has since been certified three times platinum by the ARIA with sales of over 210,000 copies. Canada, too, was ahead of the curve – it entered the Canadian Hot 100 at number 97 in June 2008 and remained at number one for five consecutive weeks in August and September, eventually being certified six times platinum by the Canadian Recording Industry Association (CRIA) in June 2009 for sales of 240,000 in paid digital downloads.

There were similar successes for 'Just Dance' in Ireland, the Netherlands and New Zealand, but it was its progress in the UK that arguably meant the most to Lady Gaga. It débuted at number three on January 4, 2009, rising the following week to number one, where it stayed for three weeks. She was ecstatic. "It's been a long-running dream to have a big hit in the UK," she told a reporter. "My fans there are so sexy and the people are so innovative and free in how they think about pop culture and music. I was in my apartment in Los Angeles getting ready to go to dance rehearsal when they called and told me, and I just cried."

The success of 'Just Dance' in the UK might be explained by its being part of a lineage of innovative electronic dance music that has always struck a chord with the British public. It's one that reaches back to the early Eighties, when experimental synth-pop groups such as The Human League, Soft Cell, Yazoo, Depeche Mode, Heaven 17 and Eurythmics ruled the waves, and goes right up to present-day exponents of synthesized UK dance music such as La Roux and Little Boots. Of course, Britain was also the birthplace of many of Lady Gaga's all-time musical heroes, such as the glam-era David Bowie and Queen, whose popularity here was – and continues to be – evidence of a fondness for, and open-mindedness towards, flamboyant, outrageous pop performers. The UK was similarly quick to take to Madonna, way back in the early days of her career, while it's also one of the few territories where Grace Jones is considered less of a novelty and more of a pioneering figure at the forefront of radical, avant-garde fashion, performance and electronic funk-pop.

Whatever the reason, 'Just Dance' caught on in the UK in a big way, to the extent that, a year after reaching number one, it was voted the track most likely to get the country dancing. In a poll carried out by an organisation called MOVE IT, the single came top, with 40 per cent of the 500 men and women opting for Lady Gaga's first hit. Michael Jackson's track 'Thriller' came in second, with 35 per cent of the vote. Georgina Harper, the creative director of MOVE IT, said: "Lady Gaga has already captured the nation's imagination with her outrageous fashion sense so it's interesting to note that she's now inspiring the nation to dance ahead of other favourites such as Michael Jackson." She added of the late Jackson, who died in June 2009: "She's not stolen Michael Jackson's pop crown just yet, as the UK still rates him as their favourite all-time dancer, showing he may be gone but he's not forgotten." Still, there are worse things than playing second fiddle to the late King of Pop.

Gaga told Britain's *heat* magazine: "It's been unbelievable the way the song has crossed over into the [UK] mainstream." In an interview with the BBC, she revealed her fascination for UK music and culture in general, including her peculiar penchant for that very British institution, the cup of tea. Speaking to the BBC from a hotel room in Canada, she said: "I wish we were sitting down having tea." When the reporter expressed surprise at this, she replied: "Listen, I love tea. I must have tea five times a day." Did she, the interviewer wondered, drink it "properly", from a china cup? "Most of the time, yes," she said. "Whenever I've got press interviews, I always have a whole tea set. It really relaxes me."

When the journalist suggested abandoning all plans to talk about music and that they discuss tea for the duration of the interview instead, she responded: "Listen, I love tea so much. When I have tea, I feel like I can think clearly and I give a real intelligent interview. Right now, I'm waiting for my tea to come upstairs to my room and I'm like a heroin addict."

But she was most explicit about her adoration of the nation during her 2010 British tour. At Manchester's MEN Arena on February 18, she came onstage to such rapturous applause, she could only just about be heard declaring, above the roar of the crowd: "I love the UK so much."

As emotional as she was adventurous, there was clearly more to Lady Gaga than met the ear and eye.

Chapter 12

Fashion – Turn To The Left!

"What I'd like people to know is that as fabulous as I may look in a magazine, it's who I am. This isn't a ploy for people's attention. This is me."

– Lady Gaga

Of course, there was plenty about Lady Gaga that did meet the ear and eye. Especially the eye. Since coming to the public's attention in 2008, she has been photographed in a staggering number of – and a number of staggering – outfits, ranging from the unexpected to the extreme, and from the extraordinary to the positively extraterrestrial.

We have seen her wearing a dress made entirely of green Kermit the frog puppets and another made of Post-it notes, an outfit comprising a hooded white leotard, a black leather bodysuit with matching space-age jacket featuring angular shoulders and topped off with black John Lennon specs, and yet another one that appeared to consist of nothing but a pair of blue Dralon curtains.

We've also seen her done up as a cross between Barbarella and a British bobby, as a futuristic Spanish widow, and as a sort of woman-sized sun complete with see-through red negligee and rays emanating from the back of her head. We've seen her in outfits seemingly made variously out of Perspex, mirrors and glass, and ones so tight and revealing they leave little to the imagination, let alone any room for a penis – she has been dogged by rumours that she is actually a hermaphrodite ever since she came to the world's attention.

It should come as no surprise, then, to discover that Gaga once declared, "Fashion is everything to me." It was perhaps inevitable that she would assemble around her her very own team of designers, one that she christened the Haus of Gaga, so named in honour of the Bauhaus (the early-20th century German arts and crafts school) and summoned forth in the spirit of Andy Warhol's Factory. The job of the Haus of Gaga has been to collaborate with her on her clothing, her stage sets, her props and her sounds, and their Warhol-esque agenda has been to provoke a reaction and confront and confound expectation.

"It's my creative team and it was really organic," she has said of the creation of the Haus of Gaga. "I was a bit frustrated at the beginning, being so new to the business and going forward with a major label. I wanted to put my own money into the show because, when you're a new artist, you kind of have to prove yourself. I was making money as a songwriter and I didn't want a condo or a car because I don't drive and I'm never fucking home, so I just wanted to put all my money into my performance."

She explained that, to assemble Team Gaga, she called "all my coolest art friends and we sat in a room and I said that I wanted to make my face light up. Or that I wanted to make my cane light up. Or that I wanted to make a pair of dope sunglasses. Or that I want to make video glasses, or whatever it was that I wanted to do. It's a whole amazing creative process."

Some of Gaga's most notable performance-art accoutrements include the Pyro Bra (basically, a bra that shoots sparks), the Disco Stick, some light-up microphone gloves, and a light-up sound-triggered microphone headset. Her range of glasses merits a chapter of its own. There are the Fame Glasses, the iPod LCD Glasses, the Razor-Blade Glasses, the Wire-Mesh Fence Glasses and the Half-Smoked Cigarette Glasses (the latter seen in the video to 'Telephone' – see Chapter 1). The Fame glasses were made out of crushed frozen acrylic to resemble crystal – they would be used most memorably on the cover of *The Fame*, as well as during performances as part of a set of crystal wear that also includes the Disco Stick and the light/disco gloves. The iPod glasses, which have enjoyed many airings in performances, videos and concert films, consist of two LCD screens taken from an iPod Classic that have been wired to display a video when turned on via a button on the top left-hand side of the glasses. The more resourceful DIY Gaga fans have attempted to make their own versions of these outlandish specs.

As for the Disco Stick, it grew out of a catchphrase used by Lady Gaga while chatting up a man in a New York bar. "I said to this guy I was hitting on, 'I wanna take a ride on your disco stick' and he just started laughing." To accompany her performance of the song, she had the Haus of Gaga make her a real Disco Stick, which she said resembled a "giant rock-candy pleasuring tool that lights up". Helped by her creative director, and some-time lover, 'Dada' (Matthew Williams – see Chapter 7), the stick was a long black tube with a light bulb and some more of that all-important crushed frozen acrylic at the top.

Apart from Matty Dada, the Haus of Gaga has always comprised a bunch of colourful characters, all of whom she was at pains to point out were under the age of 26, and many of whom were thanked on the inner sleeve of *The Fame*, bearing enigmatic acronyms such as S. 'Kamikazee' M., David 'Dark' C. and A. 'The

83

Ornament' C. Some members of the team – such as Space Cowboy, who left to focus on his own career – have come and gone. Most of them have been unknowns, although there is room in the Haus for such stellar creative types as photographer David LaChapelle and designer Hedi Slimane. Dancers, both male and female, have been legion, and they're generally just obtrusive enough – typical attire for the women hoofers is a black top, slip-on Margiela-style shoulders, tight black trousers, a single driving glove and Marni sandals. The Haus of Gaga has also provided house-room for canines, specifically Pacific Coast Harlequin Great Dane Lava and her son, Rumpus. They were used in every music video made after 'Just Dance' (Gaga even gave them alternative nicknames: Aless and Abbey Road).

Gaga spoke at length about her love of fashion and about some of her favourite couture items in an interview with *The Independent*, in which she dropped designer names like hippies drop acid. She talked about her "custom nude sequined panties with opalescent light blue rhinestones on them", her "Rifat Ozbek Italian jacket with feathered shoulder pads" with gloves sewn under the sleeves ("That's so my thing," she giggled). She eulogised about a leather nude bra that she made herself for her 'LoveGame' video and about a scene in the same promo that referenced *The Night Porter*, the controversial Italian movie starring Dirk Bogarde and Charlotte Rampling about moral ambiguity and sexual transgression, in which Gaga is actually naked under a Nazi uniform. She mentioned what she was wearing for *The Independent* interview – brand-new Christian Louboutin toeless shoes in taupe/camel colour and Capezio dance fishnet tights "[that] are very Eighties". Her diamond-encrusted Maranello watch was, she explained, given to her as a gift by her musical collaborator Akon, her producer Vincent Herbert and her manager, Troy Carter. Her outfit was topped off with a pair of vintage Versace sunglasses, but they were nothing, she said, next to the ones she wore onstage with the in-built video screens on the lenses that flash up messages (presumably she meant her iPod glasses). The oversized black patent bow in her hair was made especially for her by Christian Siriano, although her hair was hers and hers alone – a fact worth pointing out considering her penchant for wigs. "My record label have allowed me take my weft out so now it's my real hair," she explained. As for her false brown lashes, they were made of feathers by Shu Uemura, and it didn't stop there: her flesh was equally elaborately adorned, with white daisies and white roses tattooed on her shoulder and back, as well as an anti-bomb tattoo on her left hand, her own, highly personal homage to John Lennon.

"Fashion is just as important to me as the music," she told the British newspaper. "I don't want to exist to the British people as just one song. I want to be a true artist who affects their culture in the same way that I've affected American culture."

Her manager, Troy Carter, talked about his client around this time, calling her a "throwback to the days when artists were artists". Gaga was, he decided, "an iconic figure", the type not inclined to appear in public in regular day-wear. "It's not like she ever takes a day off and puts on khakis and a T-shirt," he said. "She's in showbiz, and fans have been missing people like that." Vincent Herbert weighed into the debate, deciding that Gaga's image-consciousness catered to a real need on the part of pop audiences. "She breathes, eats and sleeps being Lady Gaga," he said. "She gives the kids something new, and it's fun and healthy and positive. She does these epic videos and really great stage sets, and people appreciate that. You come to the show and see all these girls dressed like her."

There was also a sense in which Gaga was using her multifarious changes of image to keep her in the public eye. In one month alone, it was noted, celebrity blogger Perez Hilton mentioned her 13 times on his site, mostly because of her outrageous outfits.

"That rate," commented one newspaper, "is usually reserved for starlets going through rehab, involved in public breakups or falling drunkenly out of limos – and Gaga does none of this. Though she's admitted to using cocaine in the past, she seems to have realised that she can get just as much attention by slapping on a hat made of hair, without all the nasty side-effects."

Gaga explained that her shape-shifting identities stemmed from her belief in glamour and from the idea of treating her whole life as a singular art project. "I want to live the glam life, and my material is heavily rooted in that," she said, adding that sometimes the imagery she used was to provoke or disturb, and other times to comment or criticise. "There are all these places where art and self-expression and clothing can intersect. When I wore the Kermit outfit, it was a commentary on wearing fur."

She liked to offer highfalutin rationales for her love of outlandish clothes. The imagery in her shows, the outfits that she wore, were, she declared grandly, "the story of our time, of this subculture of people in New York who live and die for music, art and club culture. It's not a gimmick." Inevitably, she was interviewed by *Vogue* magazine, and took the opportunity to praise her Haus of Gaga team. "They are so talented!" she enthused, homing in on her celebrated "origami dress" by way of example. "It was inspired by a Thierry Mugler dress I liked," she said. "I'd been thinking, 'What would this dress look like if it'd had sex with a Perfecto motorcycle jacket?' And the Haus created it! They make things exquisitely."

She admitted that there were elements in what she did that were pure rock'n'roll rebel, or punk renegade, even if this was punk in designer threads. "I do have a bit of a rock'n'roll heart even though I'm a pop artist," she said. "But I'm a different kind of punk. I like clean, sophisticated lines and detail, which is why I love Chanel and Versace!"

Her interviews were peppered with the names of designers,

from Maison Martin Margiela to Thierry Mugler to Karl Lagerfeld to Gareth Pugh. Some were complete unknowns, like the "crazy Brooklyn Japanese chick" who made her false nails embellished with tiny metallic roses. When quizzed about her style icons, they ranged from Donatella Versace ("She's beautiful and Italian with impeccable taste") to Madonna ("She's one of the strongest blonde females ever – her, Debbie Harry and Marilyn").

She spoke at greater length about Madonna in *The Sunday Times* style supplement. She decided that what she and Madonna had in common was they were both "fearless" and had "a lot of nerve". She also explained that she got her fashion sense from her mother, who was "always very well kept and beautiful – she wore Ferragamo, Valentino, Paloma Picasso. Her taste is absolutely classic Italian."

Throughout all the costume changes and shout-outs to labels and designers, she wanted to make it absolutely clear that this was more than just dressing up for pleasure. Partly it came from a desire, as she told *more!* magazine, "to push buttons – I want to cause a reaction. I'm a blonde with no pants. I love that. I love the reaction it gets. I love that it shocks people, that it makes them question themselves. That I make a statement." But even more than this, more than shock tactics and the age-old desire to be the centre of attention, she stressed, fashion to her was something she felt right to the core of her being. It was burned into her DNA, it was the air that she breathed. It was a matter of life and death.

"What I'd like people to know," she said, "is that as fabulous as I may look in a magazine, it's who I am. This isn't a ploy for people's attention. This is me."

Chapter 13

Sex Crimes

"Every artist plays on sex. It's just the context, and we play on it differently. I'm a free woman, so I play on sex freely. But I'm not the first pop artist in history to be sexual."

– Lady Gaga

Lady Gaga hasn't just made a (household) name for herself making outrageous, controversial pronouncements about fashion – saying of a pair of shoes that she could "fuck them", announcing that her style icons are Grace Jones and particularly Jesus because she loves loincloths – but by refusing to conform to expectations with regard to how a pop star in her early twenties is supposed to behave, especially in this public relations-controlled age.

Ignoring all the current rules about keeping schtum and refusing to offer a PR-varnished version of the truth in order to present a squeaky-clean image, the media-savvy star has been especially outspoken on the subject of sex and sexuality, and of her sex life and sexuality.

She is, depending on the day and her mood at the time of enquiry, straight, bisexual or gay, completely celibate or rampantly promiscuous, all woman, a man in drag or a hermaphrodite. Whatever is going to get the biggest reaction, and guarantee the widest possible exposure, she is bound to say.

Much of the time she appeared to simply be giving the public what they appeared to want: bombshell proclamations designed to cause as much of a stir as possible, whether they corresponded to the truth or not. In a lengthy exploration of her sexual proclivities with Australian TV she spoke candidly, although what she said was often confusing and contradictory. First, she revealed what she looked for in a man: "A big dick," she announced completely straight-faced, sitting there coolly in her black body stocking and matching black leather cap, both contrasting strikingly with her short platinum blonde wig. "What else?" enquired the reporter. "That's it," came the terse reply. "Does that mean," the reporter furthered, "that any guy out here [in Australia] who has one of those [ie a large penis] has a chance with you?" Gaga replied, without missing a beat: "Yup." The interviewer continued: "Are men intimidated by you?" Gaga pondered for a moment before replying: "I don't know. I suppose the ones who are intimidated don't get very close." Was she, then, asked the Australian reporter, looking for a guy with very large assets? "Not looking," corrected Gaga. "I'm happy with my solitude." Then she said something really shocking, something completely counter to what everybody expected her to say: "I'm not a promiscuous girl. I'm a free spirit, but I make love to my music every day. I'm just not focused on having a boyfriend. I think it distracts you." The reporter pressed her about her supposed promiscuity, and wondered if her song lyrics led people to assume that she did indeed sleep around? "I don't really know how people see me," she said. "How would I like them to see me? I wouldn't like them to see me in any other way than my music and my stage performances." Sex, fame and music – the three things with which she had become synonymous: which, demanded the interviewer, would she rather give up? "I wouldn't give up any of them," said Gaga, somewhat dourly. "I'd rather cut my leg off." She seemed offended by the line of enquiry. "That's a ridiculous question," she decided, "because it reduces my ambitions to those three categories: sex, fame and music. To break me down into three categories like that is sad. I'm a quite complex woman..."

Indeed she was. She had, earlier in the same interview, admitted to enjoying travelling the world and "sleeping with really good-looking people". So she was promiscuous after all? Not according to *The Daily Mirror*, which reported that she was "leading by example" by choosing to be celibate because she did not have time for a relationship. Talking as she promoted her new MAC Viva Glam lipstick with another of her heroines, Eighties singer Cyndi ('Girls Just Wanna Have Fun') Lauper, in London, she said: "I, for myself, make the choice to be single at this point in my life because I don't have the time to get to know anybody. And you know what? It's okay. Even Lady Gaga can be celibate."

She added that she preferred to take the time to get to know her partner before jumping into bed. "If you can't get to know somebody, you shouldn't be having sex with them," she insisted, as though giving a talk to school kids about the importance of safe sex. "It's okay at this point, in this day and age. We have grown up and we now know that we can't be that free with your love." Enhancing the sense that she was on a tour of secondary schools lecturing teens about the dangers of behaving irresponsibly, she also encouraged women to get tested regularly for HIV and AIDS as part of the MAC Viva Glam From Our Lips campaign. "You have to be safe," she said, "so get checked. You are not invincible." She even had lots of facts at her disposal, and you could imagine her standing beside an overhead projector with a series of slides bearing amateur graphics and intimidating statistics. "Here in the

UK," she continued, "six in 10 infections are in people around the age of 13, which means it's their first time [having sex]. Seventy-three per cent of women who are sexually active in the UK have never been tested for HIV. Eighty per cent of those women in monogamous relationships are having unprotected sex, and they think it's okay because they have an agreement with their partner when we all know how men can be."

Stern, sobering stuff. Wherever she went around the world, Lady Gaga was asked to talk about sex, as though she was permanently a contestant on *Mastermind* and sex was her specialist subject. An interview with Norwegian TV was mostly devoted to the topic, and Gaga was happy to comply. "Every artist plays on sex," she said. "It's just the context, and we play on it differently. I'm a free woman, so I play on sex freely. But I'm not the first pop artist in history to be sexual." She talked about her fire-breathing Pyro Bra (see Chapter 12) and said it was meant to be a comment on the fact that female sex-parts are regarded by the media, and men in general, as "weapons". To Gaga, her breasts, like sex in general, were merely "part of life".

She was quite comfortable discussing the matter on mainstream TV – no scenario fazed her. Rather, she seemed to rise to the occasion, and the bigger the TV audience, the greater the desire to say something shocking. She was grilled by US chat show host Barbara Walters – who described her, amusingly, as a "collision between performance, art and underwear" – and in the course of the conversation admitted that she was bisexual but had only ever been in love with men. Initially reluctant to answer the question, finally she declared: "I've certainly had sexual relationships with women, yeah." She also admitted fantasising about women during sex with a former boyfriend. But there was a serious, instructional point to the interview, Gaga insisted. It wasn't about her being "artificial and attention-seeking" – every bit of her, she said, was devoted to "love and art", and she had aspirations to "be a teacher"

91

to her young fans. She wanted to free them from the misery of feeling, as she did when she was growing up, like "a freak".

Fairly freaky were revelations about Lady Gaga's morning-after-sex rituals, whatever the gender of the person with whom she had been intimate. It transpired that, following a night of passion, and just prior to her departing her lover's apartment or hotel room, she would literally leave a piece of herself behind – she would peel off one of her long, fake eyelashes and leave them on her lover's bed as a reminder of the time they had spent together. She said: "Whenever I have a lover, I leave them in their apartment on the pillow. Kind of like a keepsake."

It was debatable just how "instructional" Gaga's disclosures about her naked acid trips were, and the same could be said about her experience of sex in the back of moving vehicles. When asked by Toronto's *Fab* magazine where was the strangest place that she had ever had sex, she told them that it was in the back of a taxi cab in New York. When asked whether she would do it again, she didn't hesitate: "Fuck, yeah. It's always fun to do things that are sneaky. Sneaky sex is good." She was utterly shameless, and fearless of any reaction, favourable or hostile, to her pronouncements. Rather, she revelled in her every provocative remark and delighted in the ensuing controversy. She even fanned the flames of the debate about whether she was a transvestite, even a transsexual, in an interview with *Entertainment Weekly*. Discussing whether her outrageous fashion sense increased her sex appeal, she said: "I just don't feel that it's all that sexy. It's weird. And uncomfortable. I look at photos of myself, and I look like such a tranny! It's amazing! I look like Grace Jones: androgynous, robo, future fashion queen. It's not what is sexy. It's graphic and it's art." She went on: "I don't really think anybody's dick is hard looking at that. I think they're just confused and maybe a little scared."

It wasn't just her audience who were confused; even her pop star peers were baffled by her appearance. Responding to accusations that she was copying Gaga's robo-girl style, and with lots of photos appearing on the internet to suggest that the two performers had been "separated at birth", Christina Aguilera said, "This person [Lady Gaga] was just brought to my attention not too long ago. I'm not quite sure who this person is, to be honest. I don't know if it is a man or a woman. I just wasn't sure." For Gaga it was, she claimed, mere grist to the mill, while the ensuing furore was just great free publicity for her burgeoning superstardom.

It was also, she told *Rolling Stone*, helping to further the idea of her as a new kind of star, one who was "changing what people think is sexy" in the entertainment world. "I don't feel like I look like the other perfect little pop singers," she said. She agreed that her love life was unconventional, and she admitted that her attraction to women tended to make boyfriends "uncomfortable".

So was Lady Gaga a hermaphrodite? Or, to put it another way, did she have a penis? Even highly regarded, serious journalist Lynn Barber of *The Sunday Times* was sucked into the debate, admitting that ahead of meeting the performer for her interview, she was forced to spend hours scrutinising footage of her on YouTube for signs of a male appendage. At the height of the hullabaloo, a rumour began circulating, prompted by a grainy image of Gaga taken while performing at the Glastonbury Festival in the UK, that she did have a penis, and that she had confessed as much. Although it was doubtless just some hyped-up blogger, the quote was attributed to her and it was soon spread, virally, around the world.

"It's not something I'm ashamed of, I just don't go around telling everyone," began the 'Gaga' quote. "I have both male and female genitalia, but I consider myself female. It's just a little bit of a penis and doesn't interfere much with my life." As for the reason 'she' hadn't come clean up to this point, she said that it was because "it's not a big deal to me. Like, come on. It's not like we all go around talking about our vags." 'She' added: "I think this is a great opportunity to make other multiple-gendered people feel more comfortable with their bodies. I'm sexy, I'm hot. I have both a poon and a peener. Big fucking deal."

Penis or vagina – or both – some didn't care either way. Scary goth schlock-rocker Marilyn Manson, for one, who admitted to fancying Gaga and even showed up at one of her photo shoots to make his feelings known. As *The Observer* reported, Manson, absinthe in hand, came into Gaga's dressing room and – scanning her latest video, for the single 'Paparazzi', featuring the star "making out with a studly model" – declared that "I want to be that guy." And then, turning to Gaga, he went further, saying hilariously, and not caring who was in ear shot, "I'll give you a cervical exam." Then, more seriously, he spoke admiringly of her 'Paparazzi' imagery, comparing it favourably to the work of Andy Warhol, even surrealist painter Salvador Dali. He then compared and contrasted her with "the other girls that do pop music" and addressed Gaga's approach to fame and the shock tactics she used to acquire it, similar to the ones he had employed when he was a rising star. "She knows exactly what she's doing," he said. "She's very smart, she's not selling out, she's a great musician, she's a great singer, and she's laughing when she's doing it, the same way that I am."

Ultimately, though, Lady Gaga's focus was never really on sex or her sexuality, on men or women. It was on the true love of her life: music, which she spoke about in sexual terms. Her tour would be, she said, the "ultimate creative orgasm", while composing songs was, she reckoned, like having "mind-blowing, irresponsible sex". She explained that "writing a record is like dating a few men at once: you take them to the same restaurants to see if they measure up, and at some point you decide who you like best." She even added that she would rather spend time getting up to non-sexual antics in her bedroom than go out partying. "This evening I'll probably stay in and listen to this new song I recorded today," she said. "I like to roll around in bed with my songs and figure out what feels good."

Lastly, she acknowledged that she was fighting preconceptions and trying to create the space for women to be themselves, whether onstage, in the boardroom or in the bedroom. "We Americans are quite hard on women for their strong sexuality," she said. "But it's really who I am and what I feel comfortable with. If anything, I'm probably the only pop singer on the planet whose record label would prefer if she toned it down. But you'll never hear me say, 'Give it to me, baby'. I say it in a different way."

Chapter 14

Mission Accomplished

"My artistry is much deeper than fashion or anything like that. I love pop music, and I want to bring it back. People are truly hungry for this."

– Lady Gaga

Everything was now in place for Lady Gaga to ascend to the next level of success, a level high enough for her to be hailed in March 2010 as "the world's biggest pop star" by *New York* magazine. She had demonstrated her pop smarts with her début single, 'Just Dance', she'd aligned herself with fashion at its most avant-garde and extreme, and displayed the sort of future-sex shock tactics that would guarantee column inches across the globe. Now all she needed to do was capitalise on these early gains, prove that she had the songs to back up her controversial pose-striking, and show that she was more than just a series of sexually charged images and provocative, tendentious proclamations.

Fortunately, Gaga and co-writer/producer RedOne found

themselves on something of a creative roll, because in one week in early 2008 she and her collaborator wrote 'Poker Face' and 'LoveGame', two tracks that would end up on *The Fame* and the songs that would also comprise her next two singles.

A song seemingly about risk-taking in relationships, 'Poker Face' has also variously been said to be about the techniques Gaga would use back in her burlesque dancing days – when she would fool punters, male and female, into throwing money at her – and about feigning interest in male sexual partners when really all she could think about were women. The line, "I'm bluffin' with my muffin", which hilariously has been cited during interviews by straight-faced reporters, from US broadcast journalist Barbara Walters to Lynn Barber of *The Sunday Times*, has been said by Gaga to be about "my pussy's poker face". She explained to *Rolling Stone* that she took the lyric from an unreleased early song, 'Blueberry Kisses' (see Chapter 8), that was "about a girl singing to her boyfriend about how she wants him to go down on her". It went, she said, "'Blueberry kisses, the muffin man misses them kisses'."

Gaga stated elsewhere that 'Poker Face' was written by her as a tribute to her "rock'n'roll boyfriends" – her preference, she said, was for "boys that look like girls", adding that "All my boyfriends look like Nikki Sixx – amazing." She then told Britain's *Daily Star* that the twin thrusts of the song were sex and gambling. "It's about a lot of different things," she decided. "I gamble but I've also dated a lot of guys who are really into sex and booze and gambling, so I wanted to write a record my boyfriends would like, too."

The point was, it was designed to get people talking, and 'Poker Face' would soon do exactly that. The innuendo and sense of play were factored in from the start: Gaga clearly knew what effect, for example, her juxtaposition of the line, "No, he can't read my poker face" with the line "She got me like nobody" would have, and deliberately calculated how much furore there would be concerning the sexual ambiguity expressed in the lyric.

To ensure maximum impact, and to make sure her subversively polymorphous lyrics wound up on as many radio stations, and in as many homes, as possible, Gaga and RedOne built 'Poker Face' to be as infectious and unavoidable as possible. It featured a keyboard motif that – inadvertently or intentionally, it's not known – recalled The Sex Pistols' 'Pretty Vacant', only with a Teutonic sheen, some nerve-jabbing staccato synths, a stomping beat and the kind of "mum-mum-mum-mah"s last heard on Boney M's 1977 hit 'Ma Baker' (Gaga professed to being a big fan of the German bubblegum disco troupe who dominated the late-Seventies charts) – and that was just the first few seconds. The track proceeded at a midtempo (120 beats-per-minute) pace with all the machine-like efficiency and brutal insistence of a factory production line, while Gaga's voice had a robotic quality, as though she was enacting her 'Poker Face' for the public, and we were being asked to deduce from it what her intentions were. It was like being seduced by a sexually ambiguous android, and we were snared by its metallic hooks, notably the stuttering bit where Gaga darkly intones "P-p-p-poker face, p-p-poker face" and the robo-chorus responds, "Mum-mum-mum-mah".

The video that accompanied the song showed Gaga emerging from a swimming pool in a black one-piece (and, as ever, no pants), flanked by her beloved Great Danes Lava and Rumpus, and wearing a masquerade mask. Thereafter she is shown singing the song in various costumes, and playing strip poker at a party in a mansion. The party becomes increasingly Bacchanalian and unhinged until all the guests are down to virtually their underwear and generally dancing around, kissing and fondling each other. At one point Gaga wears her famous Pop Music Will Never Be Low Brow sunglasses while sitting beside the pool, and the video ends with her singing the "mum-mum-mum-mah" refrain. The 'Poker

Face' video might not have been quite as startling as the
that accompanied 'Bad Romance' and 'Telephone', but
risqué enough to get noticed.

"I knew I wanted it to be sexy," she said of her outfits in it, so
I thought 'no pants', because that's sexy, and I knew I wanted it
to be futuristic, so I thought 'shoulder pads', because that's my
thing."

Gaga's second single was as well-received as its predecessor.
The BBC called it "strut-tastic". About.com heard its crossover
potential, deciding that it would work as well on pop radio as it
would in "a dark, sweaty, late-night party atmosphere". *Billboard*
magazine also gave it the thumbs-up, this time with card-game
metaphors for extra piquancy: "Once again, hooks are aplenty,
with Eighties-inspired synthesizers, robotic verses and a warm,
sunny hook in the chorus, which is even more addictive than the
previous single... With a focused artistic vision, a swagger in her
interview style and, above all, a fantastic collection of diverse pop
nuggets, Gaga is playing her cards right – and 'Poker' is another
obvious ace."

Recorded at the Record Plant studio in LA, 'Poker Face' was a
critical success – it would eventually be nominated for Grammy
Awards in the categories for Song Of The Year, Record Of The
Year and Best Dance Recording, ultimately winning the last
of these. As for its commercial fortunes, they were impressive
to say the least, and helped speed up Lady Gaga's already rapid
rise. 'Poker Face' topped the charts in more than 17 countries,
including the US, the UK, Australia, New Zealand, Canada and
numerous European countries. Its American and British triumphs
were historic. In the States, it became her second consecutive
number one, marking the first time a new artist had their first two
singles reach pole position since Christina Aguilera with 'Genie
In A Bottle' and 'What A Girl Wants' 10 years earlier. In the UK,
it became the most downloaded song since the download chart's

inception in 2004 – as of December 2009 it had sold 900,000 downloads. Worldwide, the song has sold 9.8 million digital copies. If 'Just Dance' made Lady Gaga a significant new star, 'Poker Face' suggested she had the blonde ambition to seriously rival Madonna.

Rolling Stone's critics voted it their 96th song of the decade at the end of 2009."Let's (poker) face it – any decade that ends by making a star out of a screwed-up Italian girl like Stefani Germanotta can't be all bad," they wrote. "This hit defined her style of cool – both an art freak and a mainstream prom fave, singing about crushing out on another woman while she's in bed with a man. Will Gaga still be riding the fame monster this time next decade? Any fool who bets against her obviously can't read her poker face."

There was another measure of the success of 'Poker Face' and of Lady Gaga's colonisation of the mainstream and popular culture: the song, and Gaga herself, became ripe for parody. In the 'Whale Whores' episode of satirical TV cartoon *South Park*, for instance, the Eric Cartman character sang the song while playing Rockband. There was even a mock version called 'Butterface' that started circulating on YouTube, its alternate lyrics cruelly lampooning the Italian-American performer with the hot body and angular features: "B-b-b-butterface/B-b-butterface/You wanna look away/You can't from a train wreck/How can this body have this thing above its neck?/Before I turned around/You were thinking that I'm a ten/But my body's like a Barbie/And my face is like a Ken."

There was no stopping Lady Gaga now – she was like a runaway train. 'LoveGame' was her third single in North America and Europe and the fourth single in Australia, New Zealand and Sweden after 'Eh, Eh (Nothing Else I Can Say)' (it was also released as the fourth single in the UK, following 'Paparazzi'). Like 'Poker Face', it played right on the edge of acceptability –

not exactly worthy of a ban, but certain of opprobrium from all the right (in the moral sense) places nonetheless.

But whereas 'Poker Face' alluded to cunnilingus, 'LoveGame' was all about the penis. "I wanna take a ride on your disco stick," it went. As ever, Gaga was hardly backward in coming forward when it came to explaining the meaning of the song. "It's another of my very thoughtful metaphors for a cock," she said, wryly, in *Rolling Stone*. "I was at a nightclub, and I had quite a sexual crush on somebody, and I said to them, 'I wanna ride on your disco stick'. The next day, I was in the studio, and I wrote the song in about four minutes. When I play the song live, I have an actual stick – it looks like a giant rock-candy pleasuring tool – that lights up." Of course, 'LoveGame' could be read more innocently, as a simple depiction of disco mating rituals and of the dangerous thrill of teetering on that fine line between flirting and fornication – on second thoughts, perhaps innocent isn't quite the word.

Either way, 'LoveGame' maintained the pressure of Gaga's assault on the mass consciousness, becoming her third consecutive number one song on Billboard's Pop Songs chart. It didn't quite have the impact of its predecessors, and if anything it suggested Gaga and RedOne had already found a formula, with its midtempo rhythm, those trademark stabbing synths and the sort of stutter-singing that she employed on 'Poker Face'. Priya Elan from *The Times* considered it overly calculated, although *Billboard* music editor Chris Williams was more positive, commenting that 'LoveGame' had "all the winning ingredients of its predecessors: a radio-friendly, club/electropop feel, a provocative yet silly enough catchphrase and hook, and a dash of Eighties synth magic, so the adults can play along."

Although the track itself avoided an official ticking off for its lyrical content, the video wasn't quite so lucky (or rather, it was very lucky, if one regards banning and the notoriety that ensues a virtual guarantee of further commercial success), because it found itself banned in Australia and by MTV Arabia (in the US, VH1 and MTV played an edited version that removed almost all scenes of Gaga naked, and blurred the label on a bottle of alcohol one of the dancers holds).

The video wasn't offensive per se, just a little sexual, including some bondage-lite. It showed Gaga with a bunch of black dancers sashaying through a New York subway station and in a parking lot, and was meant as a tribute to her beloved NYC trash-glam super-scuzz circle of friends. "It's got that feeling of 'gay, black New York', of inclusion and glamour," she said. "I wanted to really bring forth the girl that I was four years ago." She added, in an interview with *Entertainment Weekly*, that she wanted to have a classic big dance video along the lines of Michael Jackson's 'Bad', in which Jackson negotiates a truce between rival ethnic gangs. "I wanted it to be plastic, beautiful, gorgeous, sweaty, tar on the floor, bad-ass boys, but when you got close, the look in everybody's eyes was fucking honest and scary," she said. The dancers in the video, she pointed out, were not "hot LA people that you see in everybody's video". On the contrary, they were the real deal. "Those are kids who don't get cast, because they're too fucking real. I love the imagery of a downtown, bad-ass kid walking down the street with his buddies, grabbing a pair of pliers, and making a pair of sunglasses out of a fence on the street. I thought that imagery was so real, and it shows that no matter who you are, or where you come from, or how much money you have in your pocket, you're nothing without your ideas. Your ideas are all you have."

During the 'LoveGame' video, Gaga is shown naked with blue and purple paint and glitter on her body, frolicking with two men who have the words 'Love' and 'Fame' shaved into their heads. At the end Gaga and her dancers grab their groins as they gesture towards the camera. It was all a bit much for some territories.

In Australia, the video couldn't be aired during PG-rated time slots due to some of the imagery and the "disco stick" hook line. A spokesman for MTV Arabia said, "We represent the young generation's mentality and culture so we can't play something that conflicts with that. If they can't watch something comfortably with their brother, sisters or friends then we will not play it."

Discussing the matter on Australian talk show *Rove*, Gaga was unrepentant, and said she believed she was being singled out for criticism where others were getting away with more daring content. "I happen to think people are frivolously hard on me," she said. "A lot of youth-oriented pop music is much racier than mine. 'Throw me on the floor, take off my clothes, give it to me, baby, let's dirty dance'. All these records are so provocative." In Gaga's mind, it was the context that made her music and videos different, and the way music, visuals, movement and lyrics were intertwined that made people (meaning music TV programmers) nervous. "It's the music in relation to the visual, in relation to the way I move and the way I articulate the lyrics. But if I wanted to make music to make people sing 'la di da' that would be very boring."

Part of the lyric to 'LoveGame' went "I'm on a mission", which was appropriate because Gaga truly believed she was on a mission – a mission to improve people's lives after years of bland pop pap and unchallenging, unthreatening mainstream entertainment.

"This is all part of a movement," she said. "My artistry is much deeper than fashion or anything like that. I love pop music, and I want to bring it back. People are truly hungry for this. They generally miss the Nineties and the superfans flooding Times Square, crying and wailing and doing anything to see the fingernail of a star."

It was Lady Gaga's time – time for her fame, time for *The Fame*, fingernails and all.

Chapter 15

Fame: The Album

"I couldn't be more proud of it. It's not just a record; it's a whole pop art movement. It's not just about one song."

— Lady Gaga

It was an audacious title for a début album: *The Fame*. Either that or it was astonishingly wrong-headed. Because when it was recorded, between January and May 2008, Lady Gaga had yet to enjoy any success with her first single 'Just Dance', and she wasn't yet famous, unless you count the small coterie of admirers who used to come and watch her perform at New York nightclubs.

But then, as she had always been at pains to point out, Lady Gaga wasn't celebrating fame as such, but rather the notion that you can feel famous even when, materially speaking, you have nothing. No, *The Fame* was an album – a concept album, no less – whose remit was the dissemination of the idea of fame as an intangible quality of apartness. Furthermore, it wasn't an exclusive, elite company but a club that anyone could join.

"*The Fame* is about how anyone can feel famous," she said in the biography on her official website. She added that *The Fame* also aimed to redress the balance with regard to pop music's poor reputation in the wider culture. "Pop culture is art," she argued. "It doesn't make you cool to hate pop culture, so I embraced it and you hear it all over *The Fame*. But it's a sharable fame. I want to invite you all to the party. I want people to feel a part of this lifestyle."

In an interview with MTV she explained that this singular vision of "fame" ran through the album. "Basically, if you have nothing – no money, no fame – you can still feel beautiful and dirty-rich. It's about making choices, and having references – things you pull from your life that you believe in. It's about self-discovery and being creative." The music and lyrics on the album, she continued, were "intended to inspire people to feel a certain way about themselves, so they'll be able to encompass, in their own lives, a sense of inner fame that they can project to the world, and the carefree nature of the album is a reflection of that aura. I like to funnel interesting ideas to the rest of the world through a pop lens."

There was, in Gaga's view, a disparity between fame that was deserved – by the truly special, irrespective of wealth or birth – and the sort of renown enjoyed by celebrities, no matter how uninteresting or talentless they might be. This is the area, between the two meanings of the word 'fame', that she wanted to explore on the album. "I grew up in an environment with rich girls like Nicky Hilton, whom I went to school with," she said. "They didn't do anything but were famous. I grew up and moved downtown. Me and my friends had no money in our pockets, did drugs, made demos and partied big. We totally felt famous for no reason. We were nobodies but felt like rock stars. It is funny how people define their own fame. Andy Warhol said, 'I am famous for my parties.' It had nothing to do with who you are; it was more of a choice or inner self-realisation. When I think of his work, I thought he was making a comment about our culture. Fame is an ideal and we can all get a piece of it for ourselves."

To achieve this overview of fame and attendant celebration of idiosyncrasy, Gaga worked assiduously with a variety of producers and co-writers: the list of collaborators on the foldout sleeve of the album was long, but it obviously included RedOne, Akon, Rob Fusari and Martin Kierszenbaum. This would have been the result of a directive from her management and record company, who will have been careful to ensure that she ticked all the boxes and came up with music with a broad appeal. But this varied lineup of creative partners enabled her, perhaps inadvertently, to give full rein to her eclectic tendencies. Talking after the album was completed, she spoke proudly about the way it covered the stylistic waterfront "from Def Leppard drums and hand-claps to metal drums on urban tracks". On another occasion she listed just a few of the genres on the album, including "pop, crunk and vogue – no one has been able to describe it right so I don't want to give it away." There was speculation around the time of release that *The Fame* would contain elements of glam rock, while Gaga herself spoke enticingly about its invention of a new genre that she termed "theatrical pop".

But it was the sheer variety of the record that she was most keen to stress. "I just feel like this record is really different – you've got [everything from] club bangers to more Seventies glam to more singer-songwriter records to rock music." She told MTV UK about her pride in the finished product: "I think you've really got to allow artists' creativity to marinate. It took me a while, but really delving into myself I finally got it. I couldn't be more proud of it. It's not just a record; it's a whole pop art movement. It's not just about one song."

Indeed not. The first four tracks on *The Fame* are now each famous in their own right, having become worldwide hits in the wake of the album's release, even if they, and the album, did take a while to catch on – *The Fame* was released in August 2008 but it took four months to make an appearance on the US charts and didn't really make an impact in Europe till early the following year, propelled by the success of the first single, 'Just Dance'.

That single opened the album, and was followed by 'LoveGame', 'Paparazzi' (the third single in the US but actually the fourth or even the fifth lifted from the album in other territories) and 'Poker Face'. The positioning of the first four singles as the first four tracks made *The Fame* feel, in the wake of their individual success, like a greatest hits collection rather than a début album by a previously unknown artist.

Many of the remaining tracks on the original version of *The Fame* (or at least, the second, slightly revised edition with its altered track listing and minor changes to the artwork, such as the text of 'Lady Gaga' on the cover in red) were every bit as worthy of release as the four (or five) singles in that they stuck to a now recognisable Gaga/RedOne formula. 'I Like It Rough' featured those trademark sawing synths, which in the context of this track sounded as though they had been beamed in from an early-Eighties electro-pop song by, say, Gary Numan. The lyric was typically near-the-knuckle and innuendo-laden ("I'm in the bedroom with tissues and when you're outside banging and I won't let you in..."), confirming Gaga's predilection for bad boys, and from the title inwards evinced a Madonna-esque ability to make things just titillating enough to keep listeners – and radio programmers – on their toes and maintain the idea of her as an edgy, provocative artiste.

The next track, 'Eh, Eh (Nothing Else I Can Say)', was released as the third single in Australia, New Zealand and selected European countries, and the fourth single in France. This one was hardly edgy at all: a calypso-tinged, mid-tempo ballad, it fared less well commercially in the territories in which it was selected for single release, and was certainly less well received than its predecessors.

It was regarded as strikingly similar to Madonna's 'La Isla Bonita' or the Nineties Europop of Ace Of Base, and criticised for being bland both musically and lyrically, with its tale of parting lovers somewhat inconsistent with the themes explored throughout the rest of *The Fame*. It was, with the shout-outs to Cherry Cherry Boom Boom (the *nom de disque* of Martin Kierszenbaum) and Gaga herself dispensed with early on, a showcase for her more conventional singing style, as well as one of the tracks on *The Fame* that exposed the vast chasm between what Lady Gaga was proposing – a new kind of cyber-tastic, hi-tech, future glam-pop – and the reality: nicely produced dance pabulum but certainly not worthy of being hailed as original or unique.

'Starstruck' (which featured Space Cowboy and rapper Flo Rida) was another slow tune, but it was more contemporary than 'Eh, Eh (Nothing Else I Can Say)'. With its Auto-Tuned vocal, cybernetic undercarriage and crisply clinical production, not to mention Flo Rida's rap, it recalled the twitchy beat constructions of R&B producer Timbaland. But for these reasons it suggested that the gap between what Gaga was doing and the music produced by a mainstream R&B artist like Rihanna was not as large as she might have believed.

'Beautiful, Dirty, Rich', released as a promotional but not official single in September 2008, bore the influence of New York's Scissor Sisters, being a latterday version of what a Studio 54 dance-floor favourite might sound like were the legendary nightclub to have re-opened in the second decade of the 21st century. The title track of *The Fame* featured guitars and beats and combined the organic with the electronic, the sassy vocals used to critique conventional notions of celebrity ("All we care about is runway models, Cadillacs and liquor bottles...") when really, it implied, we ought to be aspiring towards Gaga's alternative vision of fame – fame as art project, an aesthetic space in which to create and do fabulous things, without needing recourse to the usual material trappings. But her negative analysis of the empty lifestyles of the rich and famous, including the predictable rhyming of 'fame' with 'shame', was hardly revolutionary; it could have come from the lips of any number of singers. In fact, it wasn't difficult to imagine Kylie Minogue singing the track – in a way *The Fame* showcased Gaga the behind-scenes tunesmith; a collection of songs that could have been farmed out for single release to bigger stars than she was at the time of recording the album.

'Money Honey', moved along by that sawing synth sound, also featured familiar pop tropes – in the song, Gaga is faintly impressed by her suitor's fast car and even faster jet, but really all she wants is some attention and affection – that for all the radical talk about formulating a new pop prototype, was quite conservative. On 'Boys Boys Boys' Gaga the supposedly super-tough ultra-vixen, instead of calling the shots, was actually depicted as the sexily attired plaything of the boys at the bar, all those Nikki Sixx lookalikes queuing up to buy her drinks. The melody was suitably familiar, echoing old Fifties high school pop on the chorus, ideal for a karaoke singalong and innocuous dance routine on the new US hit TV show *Glee*. 'Paper Gangsta' continued the theme: an Auto-Tuned vocal presented the female lead who was sceptical of the fast life and the flash accoutrements of wealth offered by the male protagonist, who was "not interested in fakers" and had a rather different, quainter agenda: she was "looking for love".

Even 'Paparazzi', for many listeners the stand-out track on the album, presented Lady Gaga as cowed and in thrall to the song's famous male star character, intending to stalk him till he falls in love with her. Of course, it also worked on a metaphorical level, with Gaga assuming the role of the titular photographer hounding her celebrity prey till he relents and gives her what she wants. When Ron Slomowicz from About.com told her that there were different interpretations of the single, Gaga was delighted: "I'm so glad – that was the idea," she said. "The song is about a few different things – it's about my struggles: do I want fame or do I want love? It's also about wooing the paparazzi to fall in love with me. It's about the media whoring, if you will, watching ersatzes make fools of themselves. It's a love song for the cameras, but it's also a love song about fame or love – can you have both or can you only have one?" Whatever you took it to mean, 'Paparazzi' was certainly the track that helped sell the idea of *The Fame* as an album with a singular, unified theme running through it.

'Brown Eyes' was a bona fide departure from the cyber-pop template: a slow, epic ballad worthy of Elton John that harked back to Lady Gaga's pre-history as the solo piano balladeer of her New York club days. Finally, 'Summerboy' enhanced the idea of *The Fame* as a diverse delight, being a light Blondie-esque pop soufflé with a melody that evoked the halcyon days of 'Heart Of Glass' and 'Sunday Girl'.

The bonus tracks on various editions of the album included 'Disco Heaven' and 'Again Again'. The former was an excellent number, reminiscent of Donna Summer's 'Bad Girls'. Far from being forward-looking, as Gaga's interviews around the release of the album suggested, 'Disco Heaven' was as retro as hell, a throwback, as the title indicated, to the disco glory days of the late-Seventies. It was a pastiche, or an homage, but no more than that. 'Again Again' was a big, belting show-stopper that referenced Gaga's "March of '86" birthday and again (again) recalled Elton John, or perhaps Queen – the only track on the album, for all her namechecks of the British band and their enormous influence on her, to do so. Freddie Mercury would have had a field day with its anthemic chorus onstage at Wembley Stadium during Live Aid.

Despite its thematic inconsistencies and musical and lyrical weaknesses, *The Fame* was chock-full of pop hooks and memorable songs that were readily embraced by her ever-growing audience. It would prove a colossal success, one that did indeed put Lady Gaga in the position of the most likely megastar on the planet to headline the next global pop charity concert.

Chapter 16

Playtime

"Am I a con artist? Well, not so much now because I'm more well-known for my music."

– Lady Gaga

Whether or not *The Fame* was a concept album about the perils of celebrity or a collection of hit singles, potential or actual, aimed at an audience uncritically obsessed with that very subject, is moot: either way, it propelled Lady Gaga right into the heart of the mainstream. It went to number one in the UK, Canada and Ireland, peaked at number two in the US, topped the Billboard Top Electronic Albums chart and went on to sell over 10 million copies worldwide. In so doing the album transformed her from outsider commentating on celebrity to active participant in the fame game. For such an ardent student of Andy Warhol, it was fitting, not to mention distinctly Warholesque. "It's not my intention to make fun of pop culture," she told the Artist Direct website. "It's my intention to review it." Rarely in the annals of pop history has a musician so swiftly entered, then begun to dominate, the milieu they were 'reviewing' or critiquing.

Unlike a lot of celebrities who so desperately crave the media's attention, only to recoil in horror when they finally get it, Lady Gaga actually seemed to have some fun with her new-found fame. She didn't necessarily court publicity or the paparazzi, but when they came knocking, she was ready with more than just an outstretched arm and a hostile palm to communicate the idea that she wanted to be left alone. She wasn't tormented by the press; rather she seemed to be toying with them.

We had a glimpse of this after she was confirmed as the support act for telegenic R&B types Pussycat Dolls on the Europe and Oceania arena dates of their World Domination Tour that ran from January until May 2009. During the tour, the New York doll hinted that a member of the girl group had made a pass at her, although she refused to reveal which one it was. Gaga told *The Sun*: "I don't like to kiss and tell; the girls and I are very close!" She added, keeping things mysterious: "They are so nice and very sweet and I am very grateful to them because they have taken me all around the world and a lot of people found out about me thanks to those girls so I really can't say. [But] I haven't had a bad moment with any of them. I get along with them all really well." She teased, "Well, you know, I love a girl in her underwear. [And] I've been writing for them, so Nicole Scherzinger has been in my head for probably the past three months. There's something that's very humbling about being able to write for a powerhouse group like that. Probably the biggest influence that they've had on me is making me want to be a better writer for them."

Just before this tour, in late 2008, she went on the road with five of her childhood idols, the newly reformed New Kids On The Block. During the tour she spoke to an internet TV show called *On Da Grine* about the experience. "Oh my God," she said, almost fainting with delight. "I'm going to start hyper-

ventilating." She said it was humbling to be invited to perform
live as support to the Kids because she was still a new, unknown
artist. "A couple of months ago I was nowhere and to have the
New Kids be so loving and so kind and have me go on the road
with them and open for them in front of 15,000 people every
night is an amazing experience. It's been really amazing and I'm
having so much fun. I'm having the best time of my life." So
excited was she that, just before going onstage, she had a ritual:
she would meditate; although there's every chance she was joking.

She then digressed onto her favourite subject: "So much of
youth culture for my generation is celebrity obsession and at the
time I was working on this album [*The Fame*] so many young
blonde women were having their mug shots taken and they were
looking like this" – she mimed a typical vacant blonde pout –
"and I started to run with the idea of the art of fame." She talked
some more about "inner fame", "swagger" and the importance
of having "passion for your style", which she decided was
"infectious", to the extent that, even when nobody knew who she
was, "everyone wanted to know". She reiterated just how difficult
it was to achieve The Fame, but reassured any wannabes watching
that, if they really wanted it, it would happen. "I never waited for
anyone to hand me anything on a silver platter," she said. "I used
to just hustle and grind. I write music, I design clothing – I live
and breathe my art. I would not be able to breathe if I could not
do my art." She talked about her typically wacky outfit – her hair-
bow and catsuit – and explained that it was the result of calling up
her people at the Haus of Gaga and asking them, as she did every
morning, "How are we going to be brilliant today?"

One of the brilliant things she did around this time was coin
a phrase to describe her style, her art, her playful aesthetic world
view – "retrosexual". The word, she explained, came out of a
conversation she was having with a friend in the studio one day
about "metrosexuals" – well-groomed, appearance-conscious

(CAROLYN COLE/LOS ANGELES TIMES/CONTOUR BY GETTY IMAGES)

The amfAR (American Foundation for AIDS Research) benefit gala, February 10, 2010 in New York, which raised $1.2 million. (AP PHOTO/EVAN AGOSTINI)

Attending the Mac Viva Glam launch at Ill Bottaccio on March 1, 2010 in London. (IAN GAVAN/GETTY IMAGES)

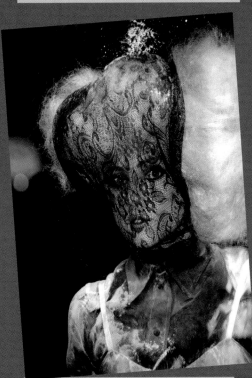

Arriving at the 13th Annual ACE Awards on November 2, 2009 in New York City, where she collected the Stylemaker Award. (ZUMA/LFI)

The lobster head-dress, with a chicken claw on her wrist, makes an appearance at Mr Chows in London, February 28, 2010. (KURT NOREIGA/LFI)

Performing at the American Music Awards at LA's Nokia Theatre on November 22, 2009, which also featured 50 Cent, Jay-Z, Janet Jackson and Whitney Houston amongst others. (KEVIN MAZUR/AMA2009/WIREIMAGE)

Onstage during the MTV Video Music Awards at Radio City Music Hall on September 13, 2009.
(JEFF KRAVITZ/FILMMAGIC)

At the 20th Annual MuchMusic Video Awards on June 21, 2009 in Toronto, Canada, with the pyrotechnic bra.
(GEORGE PIMENTEL/WIREIMAGE)

Radio City Music Hall, January 20, 2010. (KEVIN MAZUR/WIREIMAGE)

The 2009 MTV Video Music Awards at Radio City Music Hall on September 13, 2009. (JEFF KRAVITZ/FILMMAGIC)

In the audience at the 52nd Annual GRAMMY Awards held at Staples Center on January 31, 2010 in Los Angeles. (KEVIN MAZUR/WIREIMAGE)

Lady Gaga at the Brit Awards 2010, London on February 16, 2010. (JONATHAN SHORT/LFI)

The Echo Music Awards in Berlin on May 11, 2010, where Lady Gaga was a four-time winner. (PICTURE PERFECT / REX FEATURES)

Onstage during the 52nd Annual GRAMMY Awards. (JEFF KRAVITZ/FILMMAGIC)

"There is absolutely no way I would give up my wigs and hats for anything."
BBC-TV's *Friday Night with Jonathan Ross* show. (BRIAN J. RITCHIE/HOTSAUCE/REX FEATURES)

On the red carpet at the 52nd Annual GRAMMY Awards. (MARK DAVIS/CBS VIA GETTY IMAGES)

Queen Elizabeth II meets The Queen of Pop, following the Royal Variety Performance on December 7, 2009 in Blackpool, England. (ANWAR HUSSEIN/GETTY IMAGES)

At the *American Idol* Season Nine Top 5 to 4 Elimination Show on May 5, 2010 in Los Angeles.

men – and in particular a pair of boots that the friend, a male, was wearing, which Gaga thought were metrosexual and that he considered retro. So she put the two concepts together and came up with the term "retrosexual". It was a pretty good fit with the project Lady Gaga herself had undertaken – to take the androgyny of Grace Jones, the pop art playfulness of Andy Warhol and the flirty bisexuality of Madonna and bring them into the present. "It was kind of a joke," she said. "The more I thought about it – I'm so obsessed with all things retro, the Seventies and Eighties. That word just kind of flew out of my mouth one day, and it stuck with me. I often do that – if I coin terms, they'll become like the centrefold of my entire project or an entire record."

In May 2009, Gaga appeared semi-nude, wearing only plastic bubbles, on the cover of the annual 'Hot 100' issue of *Rolling Stone*. She later told *The New York Times*: "I believe in the power of iconography." She also believed in the power of poetry: she had inscribed on her left arm, in a curling German script, a tattoo of a quotation by Rainer Maria Rilke, her "favourite philosopher", commenting that his "philosophy of solitude" spoke to her: "In the deepest hour of the night," the quote read, "confess to yourself that you would die if you were forbidden to write. And look deep into your heart where it spreads its roots, the answer, and ask yourself, must I write?"

In that *Rolling Stone* cover story she talked about how former boyfriends tended to react to her alleged bisexuality, saying, "The fact that I'm into women, they're all intimidated by it. It makes them uncomfortable. They're like, 'I don't need to have a threesome. I'm happy with just you'." Gaga's sexuality was – and remains – a subject of much speculation, and again, one wonders about the extent to which it is mere posturing on her part. According to a thorough *New York* magazine investigation of her life and times from March 2010, none of her many friends interviewed for the article could recall her "ever having a girlfriend or being sexually interested in any woman offstage"; rather, wrote journalist Vanessa Grigoriadis, Gaga's decision to align herself with men and women of all sexual types and orientations was expressive of her "inclusive" politics: "She wants to promote images of as many sexual combinations as are possible on this Earth," wrote Grigoriadis, adding: "Gaga says she's a girl who likes boys who look like girls, but she's also a girl who likes to look like a boy herself – or, rather, a drag queen, a boy pretending to be a girl. There's little that gives her more pleasure than the persistent rumour that she is a hermaphrodite, an internet rumour based on scrutinising a grainy video." The writer concluded with a comparison to Madonna, the original polymorphously perverse pop tart: "That's not Madonna. Madonna wouldn't pretend she has a penis."

However, like the young, hungry Madonna, Lady Gaga had a natural affinity with the gay community. Gaga has said, of the comparisons, "I think it's great. I mean, I don't wanna be the next Madonna. I want to be the next Lady Gaga. But I'm really very flattered by the comparison. I really admire her as a female performer." She must also have watched the way Madonna built her early success upon performances and heavy disc-rotation in underground gay clubs; she certainly has gone on record as attributing her own early success as a mainstream artist to her gay fans, and welcomed her status as a rising gay icon. Noting the difficulty she had early on getting radio airplay, she stated, "The turning point for me was the gay community. I've got so many gay fans and they're so loyal to me and they really lifted me up. They'll always stand by me and I'll always stand by them. It's not an easy thing to create a fan base."

Gaga admired Madonna so much that she knocked seven bells out of her on national US TV. Only, of course, it was all for the sake of entertainment. In October 2009, Lady Gaga got the chance to face off against her iconic forebear when she appeared on America's long-running music-and-comedy, sketch-and-stand-up show *Saturday Night Live*, in a comic skit with Madonna, prior to a performance of her next single, 'Bad Romance'. Their respective generations' ultimate divas were performing on a show-within-a-show called *Deep Dish* when their supposed rivalry turned vicious: they interrupted the duet they were singing to pull each other's hair, wrestle and generally hurl stinging put-downs at each other. The show's host, played by *SNL* regular Kenan Thompson, attempted to separate the pair on the couch but the insults continued to flow. Gaga issued the first verbal blow: "Guess what, Madonna? I'm totally hotter than you." To which Madonna retorted: "I'm totally taller than you", before having a dig at her usurper's name: "What kind of name is Gaga? Sounds like baby food!" Gaga didn't hesitate in responding: "The kind of name that is number one on the Billboard chart." As the host sat on the couch to keep the warring pop princesses apart, Gaga yelled: "Stop interrupting us – we're pop icons!"

The joke was that Gaga wasn't so much – to paraphrase rock band Sonic Youth – killing her idol as presenting herself as Madonna v 2.0. And, like Madonna, Lady Gaga had a knack for self-promotion. Her genius was to use every opportunity, explore every avenue, and turn everything, no matter how obstructive, to her advantage. She almost revelled in negative publicity. Even the Christina Aguilera scandal, when at the MTV Video Music Awards in September 2008 Aguilera had looked distinctly Gaga-esque with her platinum blonde hair extensions, black catsuit and mask. Aguilera was accused of stealing her look, which led to her feigning puzzlement at this new Lady Gaga character and pretending to know so little about her that she apparently didn't even know if she was a woman or a man. Gaga basked in the ensuing media commotion. "Well, it was very flattering when it happened," she said later. "She's such a huge star and if anything I should send her flowers, because a lot of people in America didn't know who I was until that whole thing happened. It really put me on the map in a way. There are no hard feelings with Christina at all," she added. "What it showed me was, even though I've only been on the commercial market for seven or eight months, I've really burned graphic images of my visuals onto the irises of my fans. They saw a huge, Grammy-winning star who's been around for years and they recognised Lady Gaga. That to me is quite an accomplishment."

One accomplishment that the artist sometimes known as Xtina never managed was to be deemed a heathen and a harlot by the religious right. Because news emerged towards the end of 2009 that Lady Gaga was now on the Most Hated list of a controversial religious sect operating out of the Westboro Baptist Church in Kansas, known for opposing the rights of gays and lesbians, even picketing the funerals of fallen soldiers. In a notice posted by the church under the headline 'God Hates Lady Gaga', it stated that the church would be picketing "this sleazy God-hater" at her then-upcoming gig at the Fox Theatre in St Louis, Missouri. Going on to quote a verse from *The Bible* – "Thou hadst a whore's forehead, thou refusedst to be ashamed... Behold, thou hast spoken and done evil things as thou couldest" – it went on to label Gaga "a proud whore" who "teaches rebellion against God". The anti-gay cult, led by founder Fred Phelps, used further blasphemies to claim that she was busy seducing a "generation of rebels into joining her in fist-raised, stiff-necked, hard-hearted rebellion against Him" and bringing her fans into "slavery to their own corruption, teaching them to glory in their own shame". The statement finally announced, in big, bold type: "You're Going To Hell".

One can only imagine how much gnashing of teeth there must have been and how many accusations of sacrilege were hurled at their TV screens when the fear-mongers over at the Westboro Baptist Church saw Lady Gaga's video for 'Paparazzi', her fourth and final US single from *The Fame*. Directed by Jonas Åkerlund, Gaga described it as her "most amazing creative work" so far. It was also her most controversial to date. "It has a real, genuine, powerful message about fame-whoring and death and the demise of the celebrity, and what that does to young people," she said. "The video explores ideas about sort of hyperbolic situations that people will go to in order to be famous. Most specifically, pornography and murder." The violent, shocking plot-line involved a doomed starlet who is constantly followed by photographers, with scenes including: Gaga smashing her boyfriend's face with a champagne bottle; said boyfriend throwing her over a balcony followed by images of paparazzi taking pictures of her bloody body and tabloid headlines proclaiming that her career is over; Gaga getting out of a limousine, being carried by male dancers to a wheelchair; Gaga walking down a carpet with the help of a pair of crutches while wearing a metallic bustier and a matching helmet; and the star poisoning her boyfriend. Meanwhile, all around her are dead models.

But was she using the 'Paparazzi' video to make a serious point about the perils of fame, or exploiting the opportunity for her own personal glory? Around this time, one interviewer plucked up the courage to address the issue, implying that she was something of a con artist.

"Well, not so much now," she said, with a nonchalance that suggested she didn't care what people thought of her, as long as she was foremost in their minds. "Because I'm more well-known for my music now."

She was probably wrong about that, but it didn't really matter any more, and besides, Gaga herself probably wasn't bothered either way. She had achieved the seemingly impossible feat of becoming the paparazzi starlet that she had originally set out to critique and satirise from afar.

Chapter 17

True Romance

"What I'm really trying to say is, I want the deepest, darkest, sickest parts of you that you are afraid to share with anyone because I love you that much."

– Lady Gaga

Lady Gaga is so famous today that it's hard to believe her ascension to the world stage only really began in earnest in 2009. The year started with a prestigious Grammy Award nomination for her 'Just Dance' single (it eventually lost to Daft Punk's 'Harder, Better, Faster, Stronger') and ended, on December 7, 2009, with an unforgettable performance of her song 'Speechless' – taken from her second studio album, *The Fame Monster* – in front of Queen Elizabeth II at the 2009 Royal Variety Performance, which was followed by a meeting between the two great Queens: the Queen of England and the Queen of Pop (see also Chapter 1).

The rest of the year was equally eventful. On February 18, 2009, Gaga, along with Brandon Flowers of The Killers, performed

live with the Pet Shop Boys at the 2009 BRIT Awards. After a
medley of PSB hits, Gaga and Flowers joined the Eighties duo
for a rendition of their worldwide 1986 number one hit 'West
End Girls'. In March, Gaga undertook her first North American
tour, 'The Fame Ball', which received positive reviews. Gaga had
promised her fans plenty of multimedia, multisensory excitement
–"I consider what I do to be more of an Andy Warhol concept," she
had said. "Pop performance art, multimedia, fashion, technology,
video, film. And it's all coming together, and it's going to be a
travelling museum show" – and by all accounts she delivered in
spades.

She was the Zelig of pop, appearing anywhere and everywhere
that required a high-profile star, at glitzy music happenings and
more formal functions. She even attended the Human Rights
Campaign's National Dinner in October, before taking part in
the National Equality March in Washington DC. She explained:
"In the music industry there's still a tremendous amount of
accommodation of homophobia, so I'm taking a stand." She then
performed a version of John Lennon's 'Imagine', changing some
of the lyrics to accommodate a reference to the grisly murder in
1998 of gay student Matthew Shepard.

As 2009 progressed, Lady Gaga journeyed further and further
into the heart of the mainstream that she had initially set out to
"review" as a knowledgeable, critical bystander. She just couldn't
help herself; she couldn't keep her distance. Her 'problem', such
as it was, was that she had an uncanny knack for second-guessing
what it was people wanted to see and hear, and for writing songs
that couldn't help connecting with huge numbers of people. She
even struck gold – or platinum – with music that theoretically
should only have appealed to a minority, cult audience; music
accompanied, moreover, by videos whose visuals you would
normally only expect to see in an art-house cinema.

'Bad Romance' was a case in point. The lead single from *The*

Fame Monster, it was co-written with, and produced by, RedOne, and released in October 2009. It was also her catchiest concoction to date, despite being her darkest in tone, all ravey synths and pummelling martial beats, matched by lyrics that explored the seamier side of relationships. It opened with an infectious, hooky semi-chant ("Ra Ra-ah-ah-ah/Roma Roma-ma") that, like 'Poker Face' before it, recalled cheesy Seventies Euro disco act Boney M, and once again managed to inveigle the artist herself into it ("Gaga, Oh la-la") – this was fast becoming her signature lyrical device. The lyric proper began with, "I want your ugly, I want your disease", and, "I want your leather-studded kiss in the sand", both of which brought to mind the pervy S&M techno-pop of *Black Celebration*-era Depeche Mode. The atmosphere of dark desire continued with references to "horror" and being a "criminal".There followed a series of allusions to Alfred Hitchcock movies famous for their psycho-sexual subtext – referencing *Psycho*, *Vertigo* and *Rear Window* – before segueing into a spoken mid-section, reminiscent of Madonna's 'Vogue', that ushered the listener into a world of couture catwalks (appropriately, she premiered the song at Alexander McQueen's spring/summer 2010 Paris Fashion Week show in October 2009): "Walk walk, fashion baby, work it." There was even a verse in French – "Je veux ton amour et je veux ton revanche" – to add mystery and exotic spice.

Very interesting, but what did it all mean? Some reports suggested it was inspired by the feelings of paranoia and intense self-consciousness that Gaga had experienced on tour as she witnessed for the first time scenes of rampant Gagamania. Elsewhere, there were discussions of her own personal relationships and experiences of bad romance. Her observations on love and courtship had assumed the status of epigrams: "I don't need a man," she once said, using the opportunity to issue a declaration of independence. "I might sometimes want a man, but I don't need one. I earn my money, I create my art, I know where I am going. I think my parents thought I'd be married by now, but I rebelled against that whole life. I'm unconventional, I'm a rebel." *The Sun* put a different slant on the subject, one that hinted at her personal sadness, quoting her as saying: "I am single and a workaholic and very lonely." Perhaps her sorrow was due to the breakup of a relationship that she had been careful to keep quiet throughout 2009, with a former model and entrepreneur called Speedy. In the summer it was reported that the new lovers, who had met on the set of her 'LoveGame' video, had split up after photographs emerged of her in a clinch with another man at the restaurant Balans in London, where she brought her entourage following her gig at Brixton Academy. "He was so disappointed, but he is not into cheaters," said a source. "It was hard enough for them to be in a long-distance relationship, but then this came out and it was over for him."

Either Lady Gaga didn't really have the time, or the inclination, to make a deep commitment as she worked so hard on her career, or she was yet to find anyone capable of matching her own dark character and basic instincts. As she later said of the lyrics to 'Bad Romance': "What I'm really trying to say is, I want the deepest, darkest, sickest parts of you that you are afraid to share with anyone because I love you that much." Presumably, Speedy wasn't up to the task.

The video to 'Bad Romance' was pretty sick itself, and rather than showing Gaga sanitising her act as her popularity grew, evinced a determination on her part to increase her infamy. There's no accounting for people's taste for the prurient, and Gaga knew it: as of early April 2010, the 'Bad Romance' video had had over 170 million views on YouTube. It was directed by Francis Lawrence, who had worked on promos for Destiny's Child, Britney Spears and Janet Jackson and in 2007 directed the

Will Smith movie *I Am Legend*, while her creative team the Haus of Gaga managed the art direction.

In terms of storyline, it takes place in a dazzlingly bright white bathhouse where Gaga is kidnapped by a group of supermodels who drug her and then sell her off to the Russian Mafia for sexual slavery. Gaga discussed her collaboration with Lawrence in *Rolling Stone*: "I wanted somebody with a tremendous understanding of how to make a pop video," she said, "because my biggest challenge working with directors is that I am the director and I write the treatments and I get the fashion and I decide what it's about and it's very hard to find directors that will relinquish any sort of input from the artist. But [with] Francis it was collaborative. I knew he could execute the video in a way that I could give him all my weirdest, most psychotic ideas, [and] it would be relevant to the public."

Some of those ideas included a pair of razor-blade sunglasses that Gaga created, her rationale being that they expressed the toughness of the women she knew who "used to keep razor blades in the side of their mouths" as a way of saying: "This is my shield, this is my weapon, this is my inner sense of fame, this is my monster." The video begins with Gaga sitting on a white throne, and proceeds to show her with shiny plastic skin and weirdly dilated pupils that make her look like an extraterrestrial, or an android, or both; surrounded by her signature Great Danes; being forced to drink vodka; performing a lap dance; being bid for by Russian Mafiosi; wearing a faux polar bear-hide jacket; and, at the climax, in the most disturbing image of all, lying beside the charred remains of a corpse as she smokes a cigarette and her pyrotechnic bra spews flames. As Jocelyn Vena from MTV said: "The old Gaga is over, here's the brand-new Gaga: the one who seems to delight in pushing the boundaries and exploring all manner of sexual proclivities." Meanwhile, *The Wall Street Journal* noted that Gaga "seems to be one of the few pop stars these days who really understands spectacle, fashion, shock, choreography – all the things Madonna and Michael Jackson were masters of in the 1980s."

Despite, or perhaps because of, the shocking visuals, 'Bad Romance' fared extremely well in most of the world's charts, reaching number one in the UK, Ireland, Canada, Sweden, Germany, Austria and Denmark and peaking at number two in the US, Australia and New Zealand. Its performance in Britain was particularly impressive: in December 2009 it became her third UK singles chart-topper, making Lady Gaga the first female in British chart history to have three number one singles in one year, and only the third to do so in any 12-month period. Two weeks later, in the first week of 2010, it returned to pole position, making her only the second female artist of the 21st century to have two separate stints at the top with the same song and the only female artist to have achieved number one singles in both of the decades of the new century.

Gaga brought her sense of spectacle to bear on her live and TV performances of 'Bad Romance'. At the 2009 American Music Awards she appeared in a flesh-coloured bodysuit wrapped with white piping, complete with flashing lights designed to signify ribs and a spine. On *The Jay Leno Show* she wore black sunglasses and a black jacket with shoulder pads that reached above her head, while male backing dancers dressed in black suits and S&M headgear pranced around her. Her performance of 'Bad Romance' on British talent show *The X Factor* in December was especially memorable, provoking reactions that ranged from stunned silence to hilarity to awe. After host Dermot O'Leary introduced "the awesome Lady Gaga", she appeared in black bat-wings, singing the song from inside a four-metre-long giant bath full of writhing white-clad dancers, and proceeded to play the piano while sitting on an outsize toilet. Sensing the opportunity to subvert a nation, she particularly relished, and amped up, her delivery of the line "Cuz I'm a freak bitch baby", eliciting cheers from an audience accustomed to squeaky-clean, karaoke clothes' horses offering rote renditions of classic bland pop pap. O'Leary looked distinctly uneasy as he attempted to interview Gaga (who remained sat inside the giant bath), perhaps sensing that she might say something that would derail his career, like the infamous Sex Pistols swearing on teatime TV incident as witnessed by hapless presenter Bill Grundy. *The X Factor's* other international superstar guest, Janet Jackson, was virtually blown out of the water by Gaga and her bath antics, despite it being her first major public performance since the death of her brother Michael in June.

O'Leary wasn't the only one to be nervous in the presence of Gaga. Behind the scenes, *The X Factor* bosses were anxious that she shouldn't do anything too outrageous on the show, and became concerned when her directives for her performance included the building of a set based on a gigantic bathroom. Apparently, she was instructed "not to centre her performance around the toilet". Their concern was perhaps understandable: at her last high-profile performance, during the MTV Awards in September, she was hung from the ceiling, drenched in fake blood, and stabbed herself as she sang her hit 'Paparazzi'.

If *The X Factor* audience were stunned to see Lady Gaga being her outrageous self in the flesh, it was nothing compared to the shock punters got when they had the once-in-a-lifetime opportunity to see her up-close-and-personal as she went drinking in London after the show. According to *The Daily Mail*, regulars at the Castle pub in North Acton, West London, were treated to a visit from Her Royal Popness when she popped in for a drink the day after the show. It was like a visitation from a dignitary from some far-flung planet. There she was, shyly covering her face with her hand, wearing matching white leotard, minidress and boots, ripped fishnet tights and shades, surrounded by burly minders, sipping her drink through a straw at the bar, as onlookers stopped and stared, mouths agape, barely believing what they saw. Even stranger was that she had apparently gone in to pick up fish and chips for supper.

Strangest of all, though, was that this wasn't Lady Gaga's only trip to a good old-fashioned watering hole on her brief sojourn in Blighty. Because the day before *The X Factor* she had patronised the Devonshire Arms in Blackpool, in between rehearsals for her Royal Variety performance in front of the Queen. There, she was comparatively demure in her miniskirt, grey blazer and black military hat ensemble, and again it was fish and chips she was eating. Manager David Haberlin spoke in hushed, reverent tones about her time of arrival at his establishment, her choice of cuisine ("She just wanted to have a traditional British meal"), and her general demeanour as she mixed with the hoi polloi. "She was happy to sign a few autographs and have her picture taken," he said. "Afterwards she said she had enjoyed herself and said thanks for the meal. She was very polite and well-mannered. She's certainly the biggest star we have ever had in here."

It was official: Lady Gaga, pop's latest Fame Monster, had a tame side.

Chapter 18

Monster Inc

"I'm kind of obsessing over the decay of the celebrity and the way that fame is a monster in society! That's what my new record is about."

– Lady Gaga

Lady Gaga blew through 2009 like a glam hurricane in stilettos. It was as though her life depended on it, as though she thought it would be the last year of her life. She was utterly ubiquitous, but she didn't allow that ubiquity – all the tours, interviews and appearances on TV – to prevent her from doing what she loved best: making records.

And so, at a time when her peers regularly spent years between releases, endlessly prevaricating about material and casting around for the right collaborators, Gaga went right back into the recording studio and, without messing, came up with another album's worth of songs that were ready for public consumption in November 2009. Most unusually, this was while her début album was still riding high in the world's charts, a sign, perhaps, not just of Gaga's rampant creativity, but of her control over her career – most record companies would baulk at promoting a second album when there is still a first to be milked dry.

The original idea for the follow-up had been for the resulting music to comprise extra tracks for a re-release of *The Fame*, but the eight songs that she and her cohorts – RedOne as usual, plus swingbeat/New Jack Swing pioneer Teddy Riley, feted R&B whizz Rodney 'Darkchild' Jerkins, her old pal Space Cowboy, writer/producer Fernando Garibay and music biz veteran Ron Fair – came up with were considered strong enough to be issued as a brand new stand-alone collection. Gaga also believed her latest tunes went sufficiently well together, and had the necessary thematic and musical unity, to form a completely separate work. Most importantly, she decided, they didn't need the songs from *The Fame* to support them, although a *Super Deluxe Fame Monster* pack containing the new album and the début was released a month later, in December 2009.

"In the midst of my creative journey composing *The Fame Monster* there came an exciting revelation that this was, in fact, my sophomore album," she said. "I would not add, nor take away any songs from, this EP. It is a complete conceptual and musical body of work that can stand on its own two feet. It doesn't need *The Fame*." She added that she believed straight reissues of albums were "unfair" and considered them to be the result of artists "sneaking singles onto an already finished piece of work in an effort to keep the album afloat". She admitted that Interscope initially wanted her to just put out a short EP of three new songs, but that it had grown into something more significant than that.

The *Super Deluxe Fame Monster* version of the release was a lavish package to say the least. Limited to 10,000 copies, it contained the two albums, along with something put together by the Haus of Gaga called the *Book of Gaga*. According to her label, Interscope, this was a veritable feast of Gaga paraphernalia – "an individually numbered, highly stylised collector's edition art table book housed in a custom slipcase documenting Gaga's journey into pop superstardom" – that included all of the following: a lock of Lady Gaga's hair, a collectible puzzle, pictorials, a behind-the-scenes look at her creative process, pull-out posters (from a David LaChapelle photo shoot), themed fanzines (art collected from fans around the world), a paper doll collection, the *Fame Monster Super Fan Collector's Edition Art Book*, and 3D glasses to view forthcoming Gaga visuals. Additionally, informed Interscope, there would be "personal notes from the artist", featuring, most notably, her 'Manifesto of Little Monsters' as the introduction.

This extra little gift to hardcore Gaga-ites was a must-read from the pen of the Lady herself: "There's something heroic about the way my fans operate their cameras, so precisely, intricately and so proudly; like kings writing the history of their people." It continued with an allusion to her fans as "Little Monsters" and proceeded to discuss such high-minded concepts as "the theory of perception" and "the spiritual hologram".

Interesting stuff, and hardly what you might expect from, say, Britney Spears or Taylor Swift – you might not have liked them, but you had to admit Gaga's flights of phantasmagorical fancy were rare for the pop milieu. As for the album itself, the booklet that came with *The Fame Monster* included a touching dedication to Joseph Germanotta: "Thank you to my Dad, for always protecting me from monsters." The stark black-and-white sleeve art didn't exactly smack of sentimentality: the front cover featured Gaga, courtesy of photographer Hedi Slimane, as a sort of space-age Geisha girl, wearing a geometrically precise blonde wig, her face below the nose and body covered by a shiny black leather or plastic coat save for a bare arm raised at 45 degrees that created another simple, clean geometric shape.

The rear of the album featured a quite different version of Gaga: here, she had long, straight hair that covered most of her

130

face, and one eye was pouring with eyeliner, which might have been – had it not also been presented in black-and-white – blood. She looked like a sad Goth girl who had just been crying. Neither side of the album really screamed "Buy Me!" Not surprisingly, Interscope was a bit nervous at the prospect of using this artwork, and was unconvinced that this was the best set of images with which to present its fabulous new pop princess.

In an interview with *Rolling Stone*, Gaga said: "My record label didn't want to put out that photo that's my album cover, [especially the one] with the brown hair. They were like, 'It's confusing, it's too dark, you look Gothic, it's not pop,' and I said, 'You don't know what pop is, because everyone was telling me I wasn't pop last year, and now look – so don't tell me what pop is, I know what pop is.'" She insisted that she didn't want to be seen as just another dumb pop puppet, presented in a stereotypically 'sexy' way. "I don't want to do a really glamorous photo of me rubbing myself like every other blonde girl," she said. "I want my fans to see this image and say, 'I feel just like she feels.'"

Predictably, the victor of the ensuing battle was Lady Gaga herself – she ended up with not one but two covers, which delighted her because she was keen for them to convey the yin and the yang of the pop business: the stylishly slick surface beneath which lay the dark reality. Gaga used the yin and yang idea to compare and contrast the respective moods of *The Fame* and *The Fame Monster*, telling MTV: "I am ready for the future, but I mourn the past. And it's a very real rite of passage – you have to let go of things. You have to mourn them like a death so that you can move on, and that's sort of what the album is about."

Death abounded on *The Fame Monster*, perhaps understandably considering Gaga's father had just endured a serious heart operation, one that shook her to the core. "I have an obsession with death and sex," Gaga said, explaining that, in the build-up to writing the songs for *The Fame Monster*, she had been thinking about the dark side of fame, all the while immersing herself in old horror and Fifties science fiction movies. "I've just been sort of bulimically eating and regurgitating monster movies and all things scary. I've just been noticing a resurgence of this idea of monster, of fantasy, but in a very real way." She told *The Daily Star.* "If you notice in those films, there's always a juxtaposition of sex with death. That's what makes it so scary. Body and mind are primed for orgasm and instead somebody gets killed. That's the sort of sick, twisted psychological circumstance."

She had, she continued, begun to see movie monsters as metaphors for our celebrity-obsessed culture. "I'm kind of obsessing over the decay of the celebrity and the way that fame is a monster in society! That's what my new record is about, so it was kind of a perfect fit." She was so taken with the notion of monsters as indicators of various fears and libidinal urges that she had originally been tempted to conceive of each track as the manifestation of a different primal terror: her Fear of Sex Monster, her Fear of Alcohol Monster, her Fear of Love Monster, her Fear of Death Monster, her Fear of Loneliness Monster, and so forth.

To enhance the mood of dark despair, she had been spending, she explained, many nights out in clubs while on the road in Eastern Europe, where she had been exposed to dark machine-driven music. *The Fame Monster*, she teased, would see "a pop experimentation with industrial/Goth beats, Nineties dance melodies, an obsession with the lyrical genius of Eighties melancholic pop, and the runway." She added: "I wrote while watching muted fashion shows and I am compelled to say my music was scored for them." The music and lyrics on *The Fame Monster* were, indeed, rather darker than on the first album, although once again there was something of a disconnect between Gaga's version of events and the listener's. Opening track, and first single, 'Bad Romance', was heavy, albeit campily so. The second track, 'Alejandro', was anything but heavy. It may have started with a mournful violin figure, but it was really just standard uptempo Euro-pop, with Gaga doing a bad European accent for a lyric about fending off a harem of Latino hunks and the end of a (bad) romance – at best, it was sort of Abba noir. 'Monster' was about a monstrous lover who "ate my heart". It began with her warning, "Don't call me Gaga" – perhaps a reference to one of her early interviews in which she revealed that the only place she didn't like being called Lady Gaga was in the bedroom. It had a catchy chorus, but it was hardly the Goth/industrial-strength uber-machine pop she had promised.

'Speechless' was a big Seventies-rock guitar-driven ballad along the lines of 'Brown Eyes' that touched upon abusive relationships ("I can't believe how you slurred at me with your half-wired broken jaw") but was apparently written for her father – she sang him the song to convince him to have the surgery that would save his life. Produced by Ron Fair, it was recorded with all live instruments, including drums, guitars, bass and Gaga on piano. 'Dance In The Dark' opened with a series of allusions to self-abuse ("Silicone, saline, poison, inject me...") before giving 'Vogue'-era Madonna-style deadpan shout-outs to a variety of iconic deceased females, such as Marilyn Monroe, Sylvia Plath, Princess Diana and JonBenét Ramsey, the child model whose murder had so scandalised America in the Nineties. Gaga explained that it was about a girl being uncomfortable during sex. "She doesn't want her man to see her naked," she said of the song's protagonist. "She will be free, and she will let her inner animal out, but only when the lights are out." All very dark and doomy, but again the music failed to match the bleak monochrome mood, with its standard Euro-pop beats and synths.

'Telephone', featuring Beyoncé, was the next single after 'Bad Romance' and would be accompanied by a startling video that would get the whole world chattering, but as a piece of music it was less than remarkable, albeit with the now-predictably chant-worthy chorus. It addressed the notion of suffocation in relationships, and Gaga's fear, as she put it, "Of never being able to enjoy myself, because I love my work so much, I find it really hard to go out and have a good time." 'So Happy I Could Die' was a pretty Auto-Tuned ode to Sapphic infatuation ("I love that lavender blonde") and self-adoration leading to masturbation ("I touch myself all through the night..."), but it could easily have passed most radio programmers by, so agreeably melodic was it. The last track, 'Teeth', was a bit of a departure into the realms of Cossack disco, with references to her "bad-girl meat" and sacrilegious admissions ("My religion is you") that suited an album whose stylised title bore a crucifix in the place of the letter 'T'.

The Fame Monster got mostly positive reviews; arguably better than the ones for *The Fame*, although there was a sense that, now that Lady Gaga was famous, hers was a bandwagon worth clambering aboard. Kitty Empire from *The Observer* called the album "splendidly deranged". Evan Sawdey from PopMatters felt that "*The Fame Monster* isn't going to win Lady Gaga any new converts, but it does prove something to her millions of fans: that she's not complacent with doing the same thing over again." Bill Lamb from About.com gave the album five stars out of five and concluded: "*The Fame Monster* is the most compelling pop concept piece in recent memory. There are clear signs of influence from some of the top pop women of the past including Madonna, Annie Lennox and Debbie Harry, but Lady Gaga makes it emphatically her own. If this is the direction of contemporary pop, we are in good hands indeed." Jon Dolan from *Rolling Stone* was less complimentary in his assessment that at least half of *The Fame Monster* comprised "Madonna knock-offs", although he did add: "But that's part of the concept – fame monsters needn't concern themselves with originality." Best of all was the review by Simon Price in *The Independent*, which concluded: "If this is her idea of a stopgap release, we're looking here at a major talent indeed. On the evidence available so far, Lady Gaga isn't flesh and blood like the rest of us. She is made of amazingness."

It certainly sold in amazing quantities. In some countries the album charted together with *The Fame*, while in others, like the US, Canada and Japan, it charted as a separate album. It reached the Top 10 in most territories. In the US, it charted at number five while the double-disc deluxe edition including the original *The Fame* entered one place below that. In the UK, *The Fame Monster* was released as a deluxe edition only with the first album, and not as a stand-alone album, meaning it charted as *The Fame*. In January 2010, it climbed to number two and, one month later, it was at the top of the charts. *The Fame Monster* was out of control, rampaging across the planet. Nothing could stop it now.

Chapter 19

Live And Dangerous

"I want to wear a dick strapped to my vagina."

– Lady Gaga

Lady Gaga's unstoppable domination of Planet Pop was aided by her big concert tours, which ran parallel to her recording, TV and press schedules throughout 2009 and 2010. Madonna had caught her performing live at the start of her ascendancy as rumours began to spread about this new young contender to her Queen of Pop throne, and though she tried to be dismissive – she judged the show that she saw patchy, raw and full of mistakes – she couldn't help but be impressed by the scale of her ambition. Because Gaga didn't just do gigs; she staged events with the same attention to conceptual detail as her records, and with the pomp and circumstance of Hollywood blockbusters.

Her first worldwide tour as a headliner, following support slots with New Kids On The Block and Pussycat Dolls, was The Fame Ball Tour, which ran from March to September 2009 and comprised a total of 69 dates. Speaking to MTV News, she said the tour was "more of a travelling party", while her intention was for it to be "an entire experience from the minute you walk in the front door to the minute I begin to sing". More specifically, she wanted, she said, to capture the atmosphere and excitement of "New York circa 1974", with an art installation in the lobby and a DJ (whom it transpired would be Space Cowboy) spinning records in the main room, followed by "the most haunting performance that you've ever seen on the stage".

She admitted that her plans and preparation for The Fame Ball had consumed her every waking moment, not least because she wanted to give concert-goers as much value for money as possible at such a difficult financial time for the world. "I want so much to make every depression dollar that everyone spends on my show worth it," she said. "And, yeah, I'm paying a lot for it – out of my own pocket. But that's okay. I just don't care about money."

There would be three versions of her show, depending on the size of the venues she played. And, as ever, Gaga would be as involved in the preparation, in the decision-making process concerning the production, technology, design and visuals, as she was with her music and videos. The whole thing proved to be one huge creative high for her. "I am so mental and sleepless and excited for this tour," she told *Billboard*. "This is so different than anything you've seen from me in the past year. This is going to be, like, the ultimate creative orgasm for me cos I'm ready to move on. I'm not restricted to a certain structure for my show any more. No limitations. I'm free." Considering that, barely a year before, she had been "glueing sequins on $4 bras", she was now, in the wake of her global success, giddy with all the possibilities at her disposal, to the extent that she had to "pinch myself almost every day to remind myself that it's happening".

The Fame Ball shows were riots of non-stop action, with numerous sections (one called The Heart, another called The Brain, and so on), set and costume changes, and multimedia enhancements, making the whole thing seem like a cross between *The Rocky Horror Show* and *Blade Runner,* as co-directed by Jean-Paul Goude, Cecil B DeMille and Andy Warhol. After the camply theatrical intro – "My name is Lady Gaga, and this is my Haus" – Gaga proved that she could sing as well as she could stage a spectacle. Her outfits, wrote *The Daily Mail,* "paid homage to her fabulous figure". Not that there was anything conventionally 'sexy' about her get-ups. She variously wore a sculptural bustier with triangular silver panels, a dress made of transparent plastic balls (while at the same time she played a similarly transparent piano filled with yet more plastic balls, sometimes using her matching plastic mules instead of her hands), a futuristic black number, a khaki leotard embellished with crystals, and an admiral's cap and fingerless gloves, both decorated with the word 'Gaga'. Most of the time she stuck to her 'no pants' policy. She opened the show wearing a hounds-tooth body plate, sitting astride a coordinated scooter. Even her backing dancers were a space-age designer's dream, at one point clad in Louis Vuitton Steven Sprouse-printed trousers that matched Gaga's shoes. Treats included a new song called 'Future Love'.

Points were deducted by certain onlookers for her inter-song banter: one critic baulked at her intro to 'Beautiful, Dirty, Rich' – "I travelled the whole world, and when I come home, I can still smell the stench of greed," which he considered a bit, well, rich – while *Rolling Stone* wasn't overly impressed by her "tongue-in-cheek tabloid-victim shtick" and those moments "when the singer started spewing half-baked media-studies nonsense like, 'Some say Lady Gaga is a lie, and they're right: I am a lie, and every day I kill to make it true.'" But most who witnessed The Fame Ball Tour were full of praise for her singing (no lip-synching or excessive use of backing tracks for Gaga) and vaulting ambition.

Inevitably, Gaga's second major concert foray – The Monster Ball Tour, which opened on November 27, 2009, in Montreal,

Canada, and was due to climax in Raleigh, North Carolina on September 19, 2010 – was an even grander affair than The Fame Ball Tour. The original plan was to go on a joint concert tour with rapper Kanye West called Fame Kills, but it was suddenly cancelled in the wake of West's now-notorious, dramatic interruption of 19-year-old country singer Taylor Swift's acceptance speech at the MTV Video Music Awards in September 2009 (because he believed the award should have gone to Beyoncé for 'Single Ladies'). Realising that the show must go on, Gaga said in the aftermath of the scandal: "Kanye is going to take a break, but the good news is, I am not."

There were few, if any, signs of The Monster Ball Tour being hastily assembled at the 11th hour (although elements of the cancelled tour were incorporated). Gaga, modest as ever, described it as "the first-ever pop electro opera". It featured one of the Haus of Gaga's greatest achievements to date: a massive human-sized gyroscope called The Orbit. Gaga's conception of her latest brainstorm was equally grand. "It's going to be a truly artistic experience that is going to take the form of the greatest post-apocalyptic house party that you've ever been to," she said, explaining that it would be "part-pop, part-performance art, part-fashion installation" and would cover the themes of overcoming fears and evolution. She also compared the stage set to a giant hollowed-out TV.

By February 2010, with The Monster Ball Tour barely four months old, Gaga was already intending to tear up the plans and make substantial changes to the set, much to the chagrin of the Haus of Gaga. "I'm throwing out the stage," she revealed. "My team thinks I'm completely psychotic. But I don't fucking care what they think." This time, she explained, the stage set would be "four times the size of the one we're on now and conceptually, it's completely different". Her overall plan, she said, was to bring back something that had for many years been missing presumed dead:

"the idea of showbiz." Elements of her latest musical-theatrical extravaganza would include a 'keytar' – a keyboard shaped like a guitar – called Emma, which she first unveiled at the 2010 BRIT Awards, Gaga in a futuristic silver-jewelled jumpsuit with bulbs on it, a gold Egyptian-styled crown and matching bodysuit, and her dancers in either white balaclavas and white jumpsuits or skeletal headgear. There were bondage-style black leather dresses with guns, a scene involving Gaga sitting on a dentist's chair or in braids like a sci-fi Rapunzel, and another where she faked her death, as she had during her performance of 'Paparazzi' at the MTV Awards the previous September. No expense was spared, an irony perhaps lost on Gaga, who has always insisted that money has played no part in her success.

The Monster Ball Tour was rapturously acclaimed for, in the words of one reviewer, "pushing the envelope of *haute couture* and the theatre of the absurd". Significantly, although critics decided she had finally earned her performance-artist stripes, it was decided that at no point were her sheer musical talent and vocal prowess eclipsed by the sonic and visual bombardment. Canadian theatre critic Kelly Nestruck, writing for *The Guardian*, concluded: "While The Monster Ball has nothing on the great operas or the golden age of musical theatre, Lady Gaga's 'electro-pop opera' is at least twice as entertaining as, and infinitely fresher than, any stage musical written over the last decade."

Just as stunning were Lady Gaga's one-off performances. She was widely regarded as having stolen the show at the 2010 BRIT Awards in February, where she scored a hat-trick, winning all three prizes for which she had been nominated: Best International Female, Breakthrough Act and Best International Album for *The Fame*. Her performance had to be impressive to match the hype that now surrounded Gaga's every public appearance. Even given such incredible expectation, she did not disappoint. Wearing an extravagant white creation – 'dress' hardly covered the three-tiered outfit that she wore, complete with sky-high hair and mask, which resembled a gigantic wedding cake designed by someone on powerful hallucinogens – she sat at a white piano and touchingly dedicated the songs she was about to sing to designer Alexander McQueen, who had just died (apparently she was so upset over his death that she almost refused to perform and had informed organisers before the show that she would only play within a sombre set, with images of McQueen projected as a backdrop).

The songs were actually a two-part medley that began with a slow, stately ballad version of 'Telephone' that made it sound like a near relation of 'Speechless' and 'Brown Eyes'. The lyrics included a reference to London's Marble Arch in place of the one to Grand Central Station, before the line about how she had her head and heart on the dance floor provided a neat segue into the next, dramatically different section of the song: a stomping, banging electro rendition of 'Dance In The Dark', for which she stripped off to just her headgear and see-through lace bodysuit and basically terrified the crowd full of tweenies by writhing around like some mad, spurned, alien bride from a particularly disturbing episode of *Dr Who*. Surrounded as she was by mere mortals such as Lily Allen and Florence Welch, it was generally considered to be the only bona fide pop star moment in an otherwise dreary awards ceremony, one decidedly lacking in rock'n'roll antics and shock tactics.

Only journalist Paul Morley was unimpressed by Gaga at the BRITs, but this brilliant commentator was worth listening to, especially considering that, after leaving the *NME*, he helped mastermind, back in Gaga's beloved Eighties, the stratospheric success of Frankie Goes To Hollywood, an act not unfamiliar with outrage and sensationalism themselves. Gaga's performance, Morley decided, was "epic and silly, hyper and banal, expensive and tacky, self-important and resigned, and la-la lorded over by the lacy, lackadaisical Lady Gaga with her precision hybrid of shabby performance art, sentimental retro-futurism, pop music structuralism and nit-picking narcissistic nonsense." Rather than some daring future-shock glimpse of tomorrow's world, Morley saw Gaga as some kind of freakish throwback to an era of glitzy family entertainment, where thrills were safe and stars were actors playing a part, devoid of real menace or danger. "[She] takes us back to an early-Sixties world, where pop clothing was very clean, and neat, and tended to be thoughtfully pressed."

Lady Gaga, of course, sincerely believed that hers was a subversive presence in the heart of the charts, dropping bombs wherever she went. This, she always maintained, was no act. In fact, she was always at pains to stress that she *was* her character; that this was not just some hammy turn that she did for the cameras. As though to make this point, she often performed just as dramatically and startlingly offstage as she did on. In March 2010, she put on a sterling performance for the writers and editors of Q magazine. Calling a creative meeting between her people from the Haus of Gaga and the team at Q, in itself an unprecedented move – British music magazines tend to call the shots, not the artists – she boldly unveiled her plan for the front cover that would accompany her interview: to appear naked to the world with a dildo attached to her nether regions.

"I want to wear a dick strapped to my vagina," she announced as coolly as though she were ordering tea, offering the rationale that, since everyone assumed she had a penis anyway, she might as well give the public what they wanted. "I want to comment on that in a beautiful, artistic way," she said. She already had the cover line written out in her head: 'Lady Gaga Dies Hard'. Following a heated debate between Q and Camp (very Camp) Gaga, it was decided that it might be prudent to eschew the naked body plus strap-on combo and go for something a little more subtle: Gaga bare from the waist up, hands in spiky outsized PVC gloves covering her breasts and an all-important pair of trousers to keep

the magazine off the top shelves and shield her pudendum, but –
and this was the deal-maker for Gaga – a dildo causing a clearly
visible bulge around her crotch. There were hours of furious
discussion, minutes of frantic trouser-rearrangement, followed by
a final moment of silence as both teams waited anxiously for a
response from their glorious leader. No one knew which way she
would go. A British publishing institution's future hung in the
balance. At last, they got the answer they all wanted, and the April
issue of Q was finally sorted. She was happy to go with the subtly
bulging dildo idea.

"I am impressed," Gaga grinned as some of the most hardened
hacks in the business were seen wiping the sweat from their brows.
"And I am rarely impressed. I love it. Let's go!"

It was a rare instance of compromise from an artist who, it
was patently clear, was determined to do things her way, all of
the time, even – especially – now that she was being embraced
by highly suggestible and shockable mainstream audiences. But
whether she could sustain her impact, and maintain the pressure
as she pushed harder and harder against the envelope, remained
to be seen.

Chapter 20

Icon Tact

"When I was younger, I was always excited when there was a big giant event happening in pop music, and that's what I wanted this to be."

– Lady Gaga

It would be easy, not to mention convenient for the sake of the narrative, to end a book about the rise of a character as outspoken and outlandish as Lady Gaga by concluding that, after gaining the adoration of a huge audience, she finally mellowed and allowed her hyper-ubiquity to smooth away her sharp edges. But really, nothing could be further from the truth. In fact, at the time of writing this book, April 2010, Gaga is arguably the most popular pariah – if that isn't a contradiction in terms – on Planet Pop. Even in this ultra-permissive age, where celebrities are scrutinised in gynaecological detail and nothing is sacred, she has become an icon of iconoclasm – America's Fox News even went so far as to call her a "poisoner of youths". Her every utterance shrieks from the newsstands as though it were the last word in profanity, and her every move is treated cautiously as though it were compacted with seditious intent. And she appears to have no intention of calming down or letting up.

Even her more innocuous statements have about them the ring of someone who loves to cause a stir. She's the mistress of surprise. Towards the end of 2009, for example, she announced that her Woman of the Year was Susan Boyle, the overweight, brutally unattractive Scottish runner-up from ITV's *Britain's Got Talent*, who had become a YouTube sensation for singing lachrymose middle-of-the-road ballads and having a voice at odds with her unappetising appearance. "I love Susan Boyle," she said. "She has achieved more in this year than most artists will in a lifetime. This time last year nobody even knew who she was and now she is knocking the world's most established artists off the album and singles charts. I have watched the clip of her singing on *BGT* a thousand times and every time I see Simon Cowell's face it makes me laugh out loud. He thinks he knows everything but even he wasn't expecting that." Perhaps she felt that Boyle – who, like her, rose from nowhere in 2009 to achieve global renown – was a kindred spirit. She even teased that a collaboration was not out of the question. "Our styles are different. I don't know if we could work together, but never say never. It would be great to work with somebody of that talent." The feeling was mutual, it turned out in April 2010, when Boyle told Scotland's *The Daily Record* that Gaga was the person – apart from the Pope – whom she'd most like to work with: "I think Lady Gaga is a wonderful artist and completely original and I like her costumes," she said, adding that she would "love to do a duet with her, complete with telephone hat, too!"

Gaga must have come to the realisation that, when you're safe enough to be enjoyed by someone like Susan Boyle, it is surely time to up the ante. It was reported in April on MTV that her latest eccentric costume, which she unveiled in Tokyo during a tour of Japan, was far-out and freaky even by her standards. After being carried onstage by a semi-naked male dancer who appeared to be covered in talcum powder, she was revealed dressed head-to-toe in a lace one-piece bandaged around her in such a way that she resembled an Egyptian mummy, while her blonde locks towered above her head.

Gaga is a supreme self-publicist who knows the value of a stunning image and a well-judged piece of propaganda. In early 2010 she revealed that the follow-up to *The Fame Monster* would be completely different from anything else in her albeit small catalogue, even though there was every likelihood it would be the same slick, simple techno-pop as before. She talked in extravagant terms of her "new sonic energy and lyrical style" and compared herself favourably to the forward-looking artists of the Sixties and Seventies. "I find *The Fame Monster* to be completely different than *The Fame*," she said. "I've evolved, but artists should evolve. In the Seventies and the Sixties, artists evolved all the time – from album to album the music was changing, the feeling was changing, the artists seemed almost entirely different than who they were five or six years before." Even Gaga's producer RedOne got in on the act, tantalising MTV viewers by being secretive about what the duo had in store for Gaga's next project. "I don't want to say, because you always want to shock people," he said. "And you don't want to let people know, so that when they hear it, they go, 'Oh my God.'"

"Oh my God" was a fairly accurate summation of the worldwide reaction to Gaga's video for her first single of 2010, 'Telephone'. The Guardian Online announced that the video had clocked up 20 million views in its first week on YouTube and the less well-known Vevo site; by the end of March it reported that Gaga had become the first artist to reach one billion views for all her videos to date – with 'Poker Face', 'Bad Romance' and 'Just Dance' respectively racking up 374 million, 360 million and 272 million views – all of which had earned her the title of most-watched artist on the web.

Directed by Jonas Åkerlund and featuring Beyoncé as Gaga's lover, 'Telephone' – assisted by fan campaigns, including a Facebook-organised National Lady Gaga Day – was a must-see promo that created a water-cooler moment the whole world seemed to share, to the extent that it was being talked about as the new 'Thriller', the Michael Jackson video that remains arguably the most celebrated, and unarguably the most widely watched, of all time.

'Telephone' certainly created the biggest furore of recent times. There were several reasons for this. First, there was outrage at the number of product placements in the video – there were none too subtle cameo appearances by Diet Coke, Virgin Mobile and Polaroid (of which Gaga herself had recently become a creative director), which many considered was one step too far in the global corporatisation of pop. Second, detractors believed the full-length, nine-and-a-half-minute video to be little more than a mediocre amalgam of allusions to, and appropriations from, previous pop-culture landmarks of TV and film (Quentin Tarantino's *Kill Bill*, *Thelma & Louise*, and so forth). Thirdly, there were those who felt the video's more 'shocking' moments were a cynical ploy on Gaga's part to maximise publicity – a tired attempt at controversy; taboo-busting as marketing tool. Fourthly, there were probably still some puritanical types left in the world who felt aghast at some of the video's more risqué scenes (Sandy Rios, president of the Culture Campaign, criticised the video on Fox News in an interview with Megyn Kelly, calling it "disgusting... poison for the minds of our kids"). And finally, the 'Telephone' video wound people up and got them going simply because it was a riot of sensational(ist) images – Matt Donnelly from *Los Angeles Times* called it a "visual feast, packed with fantastic fashion, girl fights, poisoned diner food, an army of headpieces and lots of

Gaga goodness". He neglected to mention the lesbian kisses, the formation writhing around the jail cells in bikinis, the Sapphic crotch-rubbing, and the expletives deleted from Beyoncé, but still… Gaga was just happy to revel in the commotion. In an interview on KIIS-FM with Ryan Seacrest, she said: "What I like about it is it's a real, true pop event, and when I was younger, I was always excited when there was a big giant event happening in pop music, and that's what I wanted this to be."

Whatever your view of it, the video fulfilled its purpose and helped catapult the 'Telephone' single to the top of the world's charts. On March 22, 2010 it reached number one in the UK, making it Gaga's second consecutive British chart-topper and her fourth in total. It reached number three on the Billboard Hot 100, making it her sixth straight single to reach the Top 10, and it made number one on the Pop Songs chart, her sixth consecutive single to do so, equalling Beyoncé's and Mariah Carey's record for the most number ones since the radio airplay chart began in 1992.

By the spring of 2010 Lady Gaga had become a gift to newspaper editors, as well as something of a scandal-magnet. Not all of the attention she received was favourable. In mid-March, it was reported that her early collaborator and producer, Rob Fusari, had filed a $30.5m lawsuit against her. The 41-year-old claimed that she had denied him royalty shares for the music on *The Fame* in which he had a hand (he is credited for a number of songs on the début album). He was also, he furthered, the person responsible for her change of name from Stefani Germanotta to Lady Gaga, and was instrumental in facilitating her record deal with Interscope, and so played an active role in "radically reshaping her approach" to her career.

Fusari intimated that he and Gaga were romantically involved when they launched their Team Love Child venture in May 2006, but that when their personal relationship fizzled out, their business relationship also came shuddering to a halt. Fusari alleged that he had been denied a 20% share of song royalties and shares of merchandising sales, acknowledging that he had received about $611,000 from Gaga but disputing that this was the full share to which he was entitled. A representative for Lady Gaga had no comment to offer on the lawsuit.

Fusari spoke at length to *Billboard* magazine just as news emerged of his lawsuit against his former charge and paramour – the Fame Monster to his Dr Frankenstein, as the magazine put it. He revealed that he had not been invited to work on her next album. Asked whether he and Gaga were still friends, he replied, "I don't know. I feel like I may have been demoted to . . . what would be one level beneath friend?" "Professional acquaintance?" suggested *Billboard* journalist Craig Marks. "Yeah, there you go," said Fusari. "That's it." Marks asked Fusari why he believed he was no longer involved in Gaga's career, and what exactly happened to curtail that involvement, but he didn't know the answer. "I can't figure it out," he said, "and I won't ask. I don't know if I said something or did something. I don't know." He did say, however, that he was happy to have played his part in the irresistible rise of Gaga, that he felt "a huge sense of accomplishment that we built something together", and that the pair had seen each other briefly at the Grammy Awards, where they congratulated each other on their respective achievements. "I'm extremely happy for her," he said. The case was ongoing at the time of this book going to press.

There was fuss at a more local level in April when Cole Goforth, a 15-year-old high school student from Tennessee, was sent home because his Lady Gaga T-shirt was said to be causing a "disruption". The T-shirt in question was an item bought at one of her Monster Ball Tour dates, and featured the words "I ♥ Lady GAY GAY" emblazoned across the chest. The incident attracted the attention of local news teams and websites such as The Advocate, which alleged that the school had violated the boy's freedom of speech. As for the teenager, he said via Twitter: "Individuality, self-expression, and truly being comfortable with yourself is something that runs so deep to me, I could cry talking about it." He continued: "I don't think my sexuality is widely accepted around here, so of course they are going to single me out." When Gaga heard about the incident, she got tweeting herself to defend the young fan. With nearly three-and-a-half million followers on Twitter, it was inevitable that her grammatically and syntactically sloppy though heartfelt response would considerably increase media interest in the story. "Been in the studio for days and hours of record after record, and when I hear that a little monster was discriminated against* BY TEACHERS

Thank u for wearing your tee-shirt proud at school, you make me so proud, at the monsterball, you are an inspiration to us all. I love you.X

It reminds me of my commitment + love for u, and the deep unconditional devotion I feel to write music that will liberate you from prejudice."

She might have felt less deep, unconditional love for radical Sri Lankan pop artist M.I.A., who in April was widely reported as having criticised Gaga in British music weekly *NME*. It was a sustained attack that articulated many of the doubts people in the industry had had about Gaga for a while. "People say we're similar, that we both mix all these things in the pot and spit them out differently, but she spits it out exactly the same!" said the singer, born Mathangi 'Maya' Arulpragasam, who maintained that Gaga was a highly derivative artist who based her music and image on many, including herself. "None of her music's reflective of how weird she wants to be or thinks she is. She models herself on Grace Jones and Madonna, but the music sounds like 20-year-old Ibiza music, you know? She's not progressive, but she's a good mimic. She sounds more like me than I fucking do! That's a talent and she's got a great team behind her, but she's the industry's last stab at making itself important – saying, 'You need our money behind you, the endorsements, the stadiums.' Respect to her, she's keeping 100,000 people in work, but my belief is: do it yourself."

Then Grace Jones herself, one of her all-time heroines and her clearest avant-fashion role model, decided to join in with the Gaga-bashing. In an interview with Simon Hattenstone of *The Guardian*, when asked whether a team-up with Gaga was likely, Jones replied: "I don't play with other acts as a rule." When pushed to offer an opinion on her, the Jamaican diva said coolly: "I really don't think of her at all. I go about my business." Had Lady Gaga, teased Hattenstone, copied her? "Well, you know," she began, "I've seen some things she's worn that I've worn, and that does kind of piss me off." Did Jones consider her talented? "I wouldn't go to see her," she answered. Finally, when asked whether Gaga had approached her with regard to a collaboration, Jones said: "Yes, she did, but I said no," adding: "I'd just prefer to work with someone who is more original and someone who is not copying me, actually."

Of course, there were far fewer Gaga haters than there were fans – in all corners of the globe. A measure of the extent to which she had impacted on the world's consciousness came in April when it was reported by The Times Online that "Oh My Lady Gaga!" had replaced "Oh My God!" among hip young Chinese internet users looking for novel ways to express surprise. "The phrase has become all the rage in text messages and in chatrooms, where scattering conversations with fashionable – and widely understood – English slang or acronyms is the acme of cool", went the article, which also pointed out that the trend was causing some anxiety among academics and Chinese authorities concerned about the pernicious influence of foreign neologisms on the traditional native tongue.

Gaga could boast fans in far-flung places. She had some pretty high-profile ones, too, including Sir Elton John and the producers of the James Bond movie franchise. She was rumoured to be in the running to sing, and possibly even write, the next James Bond theme, an accolade reserved for pop's biggest names and one previously enjoyed by the likes of Paul McCartney, Carly Simon, Duran Duran and A-Ha. Production had yet to start on the movie, which would see Daniel Craig return in the role of superspy 007, but already Gaga's name had been mooted as a likely candidate for the prestigious theme tune. Sir Elton, who sang with Gaga on a version of 'Speechless' at the Grammy Awards earlier in the year, was delighted, and implied that the Bond theme may even be a duet. "I'm really pleased that Lady Gaga is up for the theme tune," John told *People* magazine. "She's fantastic. It would be amazing to do a duet."

Slightly less joyous were the reports, in the April 10-16 2010 issue of *heat* magazine, about a "tired, hysterical, obsessed" Lady Gaga. She was, it was alleged, "stressed out" by Rob Fusari's impending $30.5 million lawsuit and had been "plaguing" her ex-boyfriend Speedy with constant "hysterical and tearful" phone calls, messages and late-night texts in an effort to win him back: "One is refusing to take the singer back, while the other is driving her to the brink of financial meltdown," wrote the magazine of her two ex-boyfriends, suggesting that each crisis was making the other worse. "The trauma of the situation [with Fusari] has made Gaga more desperate to get back together with Speedy, who she thinks will provide a shoulder to cry on." The magazine also warned about the effect of all this on Gaga's mental and physical health, saying that "the stress and heartbreak" had "left her looking gaunt, unhappy and haunted recently".

Meanwhile, *Look* magazine, "Britain's Best-Selling Fashion Weekly", featured Lady Gaga on the cover, next to the headline: "Why I'm afraid my family will disown me". Inside, it was reported that Gaga was feeling "torn" between her family and her sexuality, claiming that she was unable to decide whether to be with a man or a woman. "She's scared that if she falls for a woman," said a source, "her family will reject her, because ultimately they want her to settle down with a man." The magazine also alleged that her relationship with ex-boyfriend Speedy had broken down because of her desire to eschew conventional courtship and date other men and women while she was still seeing him. The source claimed that, "For all Gaga's success, her love life is a mess", and that she was "throwing herself into her work to the point of exhaustion because of a crippling inner turmoil".

Was Lady Gaga really heading for a fall, or riding high? One suspected that there were elements of truth in all the stories about her, but that ultimately, to Gaga, it didn't matter anyway because she was where she wanted to be: on top of the world. In Britain, she was a household name, an unavoidable feature of the cultural landscape. In April 2010, she was back at the top of the UK album chart for the fourth time with *The Fame* (there was also news of a remix version of the album, due in May, featuring reworkings of her songs by Pet Shop Boys, Marilyn Manson, Alphabeat and Madonna's producer Stuart Price). There was even an episode of Britain's favourite soap opera, *EastEnders*, broadcast on April 18, in which two child characters dressed up as junior Lady Gagas and cavorted about to 'LoveGame', only to be interrupted by a horrified Phil Mitchell (played by Steve McFadden), at which the under-age pair turned to the thunderstruck hard-man and asked: "What's a disco stick?"

Of course, Lady Gaga would never have settled for merely colonising one tiny island. It had been from the outset her intention to become the biggest pop star on the planet, and by 2010 she had achieved exactly that. It was an exalted position that came with its own set of problems, but Gaga knew that she would overcome them: she had the blonde ambition. She knew deep down that anybody, in theory, could be where she was today, but not everyone had the necessary qualities, that special magic essence, that pushed them to sustain it over the distance. To Lady Gaga, global domination was second nature.

As she told *New York* magazine in April: "Everyone can access the parts of themselves that are great. I'm just a girl from New York City who decided to do this, after all. Rule the world! What's life worth living if you don't rule it?"